*Police
Driving
Techniques*

Police Driving Techniques

Anthony Scotti

*Scotti School
of Defensive Driving*

A Brady Book
Prentice Hall
Englewood Cliffs, N.J. 07632

Library of Congress Cataloging-in-Publication Data

Scotti, Anthony J.
  Police driving techniques.

  Bibliography: p. 181.
  Includes index.
  1. Police pursuit driving. 2. Police patrol.
3. Traffic safety. I. Title.
HV8080.P9.S39 1988   363.2'32   87-12468
ISBN 0-89303-679-X

Editorial/production supervision
  and interior design: Ed Jones
Cover design: Amy Scerbo
Manufacturing buyer: Margaret Rizzi

 © 1988 by Prentice-Hall, Inc.
A Division of Simon & Schuster
Englewood Cliffs, NJ 07632

Printed in the United States of America

10 9 8 6 7 5 4 3 2 1

ISBN 0-89303-679-X 025

PRENTICE-HALL INTERNATIONAL (UK) LIMITED, *London*
PRENTICE-HALL OF AUSTRALIA PTY. LIMITED, *Sydney*
PRENTICE-HALL CANADA INC., *Toronto*
PRENTICE-HALL HISPANOAMERICANA., S.A., *Mexico*
PRENTICE-HALL OF INDIA PRIVATE LIMITED, *New Delhi*
PRENTICE-HALL OF JAPAN, INC., *Tokyo*
PRENTICE-HALL OF SOUTHEAST ASIA PTE. LTD., *Singapore*
EDITORA PRENTICE-HALL DO BRASIL, LTDA., *Rio de Janeiro*

Dedicated to . . .
my wife, *Judy*, and
my daughter, *Toni-Ann*

Contents

Foreword

In *Police Driving Techniques*, Tony Scotti shares the unique driving methods of the Scotti School of Defense Driving, police driving, and antiterrorist techniques that have been taught to thousands of police officers, police academy driving instructors, and military personnel throughout the world. Actively involved in extensive driving safety research since 1976, Mr. Scotti has provided here an authoritative and comprehensive volume that covers all the important aspects of safe police driving. In these pages, he not only discusses what to do and what not to do, but also provides practical explanations of the reasoning behind his techniques.

Police officers will find here a host of facts and insights that will ultimately give them more personal control over their vehicles— control in any situation. They'll learn to recognize the five major accident situations and the human and mechanical failures that usually cause them. Officers will see how driving is a state of mind, will understand the necessity of both mental and physical readiness, and will learn the adverse effects of fatigue and stress. Further, they'll come to know the basics of vehicle dynamics—how the vehicle itself responds to the driver's input—and why the vehicle sometimes does what it wants to do, and not what the driver wants it to.

Some may feel that "driving is driving." After reading *Police Driving Techniques*, however, they'll truly appreciate the differences between "regular" vehicles and police vehicles—and they'll gain insight into the finer points of vehicle control in everyday driving (timing, maneuvering, spotting hazards before they become accidents), and in emergency situations (such as when there are five seconds or less between the driver and a potentially serious accident). Here Mr. Scotti shows how the driver must operate the controls with precision, with accuracy, and in the proper sequence.

A whole host of extenuating circumstances affects both routine and emergency driving—road conditions, weather effects, vehicle condition (tires, brakes, etc.), night driving, high-speed driving (both emergency and pursuit), and the legal liabilities involved. Police officers will find all these important aspects covered in detail.

Police Driving Techniques also gives officers a chance to test and evaluate their own police driving IQ. Included are basic driving exercises and test methods used by all police emergency and vehicle operator courses to teach effective driving techniques.

Police officers from all areas of the country—from rural departments to large urban police forces—will benefit from this book. In over 40 percent of all automobile accidents, the drivers never realized they were in trouble until they heard the screech of tires and the crunch of steel—and police officers have been no exception. *Police Driving Techniques* will help significantly reduce officers' vulnerability to be taken by surprise—not by criminals, but by their own vehicles.

> Deputy Superintendent Robert O'Toole
> Chief Instructor
> Boston Police Academy

Preface

The National Safety Council estimates that automobile accidents account for approximately one-third of all the work-related fatalities in the U.S. today. Because law-enforcement officers spend most of their time on patrol in various types of vehicles, the danger they face from automobile accidents is especially grave.

Certain types of driving situations produce most police accidents. Officers must be aware of these situations and of what they can do to avoid them. Given the nature of their work, police officers cannot always drive in a way that leaves them immune to a dangerous driving situation. Thus, it is vital for law-enforcement officers to understand the events leading up to accidents and what they can do to help prevent the accident from happening.

This is a far more difficult task for police than it is for the average citizen. Police officers are obliged to drive in all types of weather and on all types of roads. They must be trained to analyze accurately the situations in which they find themselves and drive within the limits of safety.

High-speed pursuits pose an especially dangerous problem. Officers must learn how to minimize the dangers on pursuits, to decrease the possibility of a tragic accident, to avoid needless injuries to bystanders, and to decrease the costly lawsuits that inevitably follow.

This book is written for police officers, and it is their input that made the book possible. Many others contributed, and I'd like to take this opportunity to thank them. Judy Scotti and Cathy

McMahon spent a great deal of time assembling the materials for the text. Goodyear Tire & Rubber Company made its engineers available for our many questions on police-vehicle tires. Thomson Speedway graciously allowed us to use its facilities for hours of endless testing. The Port Authority of New York and New Jersey as well as the Madison, N.J., Police Department helped us with photos and lent valuable moral support. I would especially like to thank Chief Capen of the Madison Police Department for offering helpful suggestions. Thanks also to the Boston Police Department for its help in the research and development of this book, and to Deputy Superintendent Robert O'Toole of the Boston Police Department for his assistance and contribution. Last, but certainly not least, I would like to thank all of the Scotti School instructors.

Anthony Scotti
Scotti School of Defensive Driving

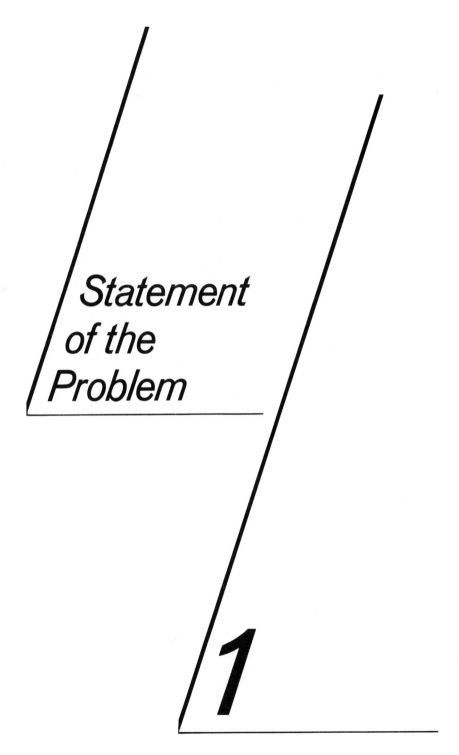

Statement of the Problem

1

The police officer's level of exposure to potential auto accidents is far higher than that of the average citizen. More than likely, an officer's shift is spent entirely on the road, and the dangers of this increased exposure are compounded by the fact that officers are routinely required to drive at night, or in other conditions in which reduced visibility increases the probability of an accident. The adverse weather conditions civilians can avoid by simply staying at home are more often than not the very conditions that bring an officer to work. They can't refuse to go out in bad weather. That part of their job is not optional.

A perfect example of this kind of increased accident potential is a late-night call during a blinding rainstorm that requires an officer to make a high-speed run. Not many people are *required* to drive in these conditions; not even professional racing drivers have to go out in the rain.

Beyond this aggravated exposure to danger while performing the public safety aspect of their job are the extraordinary demands placed upon police drivers by the law-enforcement demands of police work. Occasionally police must pursue a driver who will take risks that endanger the lives of innocent bystanders. Police drivers are often required to make high-speed runs to accident sites. More often than not, these accidents are accompanied by traffic jams, crowds of spectators, or other factors that present a high potential for injuries or worse. Police sometimes become impromptu ambulance drivers, quickly transporting the injured to hospitals when no other transport is available.

The bottom line is simply this: Police officers must have a high level of endurance behind the wheel, along with driving skills few other occupations require.

As a police officer, you spend about 65 percent of your duty time in your police cruiser. The cruiser is your mobile office, your place of work. If not used properly, your vehicle can be a death trap—an accident looking for a place to happen.

Statistics indicate that as a law-enforcement officer, you are more likely to be injured in a vehicle accident than by gunshot wounds or any other form of violence you will encounter in the line of duty. While driving under stress or adverse conditions, you and your department cannot afford to look bad. The public demands that you be a good driver, that you drive in a safe and controlled manner, no matter what the conditions. Your job as a police officer is to serve and protect. Thus, it is vital that you set a good example when behind the wheel.

MOTOR VEHICLE ACCIDENTS

Of course, motor vehicle accidents don't just happen to officers. They are a tremendous societal problem and place a heavy burden on everyone. In 1980 alone, motor vehicle accidents in the U.S. killed over 51,000 people and injured 4 million others. The loss of life and injuries resulting from these accidents led to a tremendous amount of personal grief and to economic hardship for the survivors and families of those involved. No price tag can be put on suffering, and unless the unthinkable happens to you, the statistics involved are about as exciting as watching paint dry.

However, the hard world of statistics can reveal the economic and human costs of automobile accidents. Hence, it is vital to understand these costs because, as members of society, we all bear them.

According to the National Safety Council, auto accidents cost the nation $43.3 billion a year. That is nearly equal to work and home accidents combined, which are the second and third biggest causes, respectively, of all the accidents annually in the U.S.

Motor vehicle accidents are also the fourth leading cause of death in America. Only heart disease, cancer, and stroke claim more lives. As a police officer, you are therefore exposed to not just the health threats everyone else faces, but you face added danger in the form of increased auto accident exposure.

Another report, also by the National Safety Council, indicates an annual $57.7 billion loss due to highway deaths. This figure represents $3.3 billion in medical costs, $21 billion in property loss, $14.7 billion worth of lost productivity, and another $18.7 billion in other costs. These accidents resulted in more than 3 million people a year missing 3.7 days of work due to auto accidents, and another 350,000 hospitalized for severe head injuries.

But these are all just numbers; impressive numbers, granted, but still numbers. They do not reflect the personal tragedies that you see every day as part of your job. What we aim for in this book is to keep you and your fellow officers from becoming tragedies yourselves.

You probably know an officer who has been involved in some sort of highway tragedy. If it's never happened to you, you can never understand the pain of being accused of causing injury, especially to an innocent bystander whose car was hit by a vehicle you were pursuing. Imagine taking the witness stand in court, testifying, trying to explain to a jury that you were just doing what you're paid to do—that you didn't mean for the accident to happen. No matter how tough-minded you think you are, it hurts.

You can best serve yourself and the public when you follow some simple rules and operate your police vehicle in a safe and efficient manner.

POLICE ACCIDENTS

Most police administrators agree that motor vehicle accidents are the number-one cause of police injuries. These accidents drain the budgets of police departments, both large and small. Unfortunately, too many administrators feel that these accidents are just another cost of doing business—a bad attitude to develop in terms of both liability and safety. Police officers are required to drive under conditions requiring a high degree of skill and knowledge. Officers need to have:

1. A basic understanding of the vehicle's capabilities and also what the vehicle is *not* capable of. It's comforting to know that your cruiser takes 60 feet to stop at 30 mph, especially if there is a truck stopped 55 feet in front of you at the moment.
2. Thorough knowledge of the motor vehicle laws. It's amazing how many officers think they can arbitrarily violate traffic laws.
3. Knowledge of how accidents happen and the types of environments in which they are likely to occur. Because of the nature of the job, you and your cruiser must often go into harm's way; for instance, pursuing a vehicle down a busy street at rush hour.
4. Reasonable reaction times due to good physical condition.
5. A good attitude toward driving and thorough knowledge of your departmental regulations regarding driving.
6. Mature judgment.
7. Proven skill in controlling a vehicle in an emergency.

Police Statistics

Because of the specialized nature of police driving, it really should not be compared to the driving performance of the general public. Unfortunately, it often is. And just how do officers compare? According to the National Safety Council, police vehicles were involved in 12.78 accidents per million miles driven in 1980.[1] Passenger cars are involved in 4.1 mishaps per million miles; trucks, 7.95; and buses, 12.47.

[1] *Accident Facts*, 1984 ed. (Chicago: National Safety Council), p. 64.

This means the accident rate for police officers is a little more than three times that of the general public, about 1.5 times that of truck drivers, and, surprisingly, about the same as that of bus drivers. Examining these numbers a little more closely reveals some interesting discoveries. If that rate of 12.78 accidents per million miles is broken down by types of public-safety departments and by types of vehicles, we find the following:

1. 23.6 accidents per million miles for municipal vehicles.
2. 4.82 accidents per million miles for state patrol vehicles.
3. 30.78 accidents per million miles for two-wheeled motorcycles.
4. 21.54 accidents per million miles for three-wheeled motorcycles.

At first glance, it may seem that police officers driving municipal vehicles have more of a safety problem than state police, that municipal police are little more than accidents looking for a place to happen. Municipal police do have five times as many accidents as the general public. State police have roughly the same accident rates as the general public. What is important to note here isn't an implied level of driving competence or incompetence. In this case the numbers reveal the truth about the differences in driving environments experienced by the two groups. A world of difference exists between a 50-mph pursuit through city streets and an 80-mph pursuit down a four-lane, divided highway. With practically no threat of pedestrian interference, the highway chase is far safer, at least for bystanders. However, a high-speed chase is never entirely safer for the occupants of the vehicles involved. A pursuit through the streets of a large city carries with it the potential for an accident at every intersection.

Therefore, comparing municipal police officers' driving records to those of a highway or state patrol isn't really fair, or very meaningful. A far more accurate comparison would result from comparing the records of officers driving in roughly the same environment and the same number of hours. In a comparison of professional drivers operating vehicles in comparable cities eight hours a day, an entirely different picture emerges. In this case, the accident rates are:

• Common carriers—37.76 accidents per million miles.
• Intercity buses—36.89 accidents per million miles.
• Private carriers—15.03 accidents per million miles.

This is a far more accurate comparison. When compared to these groups, police have a lower accident rate than either common carriers or intercity buses. And, once more, we must consider the conditions under which police operate vehicles. It simply is not accurate to compare drivers who operate vehicles in short spurts on four-lane, divided highways with those who must drive for six to eight hours at a stretch on two-lane, high-volume roads.

If all these numbers seem a little intimidating, consider the fact that the overall accident rate for police officers is decreasing. In 1979, the accident rate was 17.88 per million miles driven, compared to the 1984 rate of 12.78, a significant improvement of about 28 percent.[2]

From both studies such as these and from popular TV shows, it's easy to see why police officers have a reputation of being reckless drivers, but that's simply not true. Many factors contributing to police accident rates are not taken into consideration:

1. Because the statistics are presented as miles driven, accident rates are somewhat equalized. Some police duties and routine patrol procedures require officers to get in and out of the car a lot. Other missions require a lot of steady driving. If you've ever driven eight hours at a stretch, you know how grueling it can be. On the other hand, if you've ever put in eight hours' worth of driving with regular stops for coffee and a leg-stretch, you know how relatively easy it can be.

2. Droning around the city in a police cruiser for six hours on a slow night can have much the same effect as taking a sleeping pill. Because of the demands of the job, police are often required to drive when tired. In later chapters, we'll find out why this is especially dangerous.

3. As we've said, police don't get to choose the weather they drive in. The driving environment for police officers is nothing like that of civilian drivers.

4. There is nothing like zooming through a 25-mph zone at 70 mph to add a little excitement to your life. Police are sometimes required to drive that way in the performance of their duties. Granted, there are many arguments against the high-speed pursuit, and we'll look at some of them in another chapter.

Although unsubstantiated by any statistical data I know of, it appears reasonable to say that the police accident rate is three times that of the public's because police are faced with three times the

[2] Ibid., p. 56.

danger as the public. However, this does not absolve police of the responsibility of being safe drivers. In fact, it is the officer's job to be an above-average driver.

Police Pursuit

No type of accident receives more public attention than the accident incurred in a high-speed pursuit. There is surprisingly little research data on high-speed pursuit, surprising because this type of accident deserves a great deal of attention.

According to the U.S. Department of Transportation (DOT), between 50,000 and 500,000 hot pursuits occur in the U.S. annually. Some 6,000 to 8,000 of these result in crashes of some kind or another. Between 300 to 400 people are killed in these crashes, and some 2,500 to 5,000 injured.

In another study, the Physicians for Automotive Safety (PAS) found that out of a case-study group of 512 pursuits, 118 fatalities resulted, as did 272 major injury cases and 237 minor injury cases. Comparing the DOT and PAS studies, a wide disparity becomes apparent. About all these two studies prove for certain is that more research needs to be done.

No matter how you look at it, driving a car at high speeds through crowded city streets is at best a dangerous proposition, yet it is something a police officer may be required to do at a moment's notice.

Department Accident Rates

We can compare your accident record or your department's accident record to the average accident rate by looking at some simple statistics:

- 167.7 million motor vehicles were registered in the U.S. in 1984.
- 152 million people were licensed drivers in the U.S.
- 18.3 million accidents occur each year.

Some quick arithmetic shows us that there are 0.12 accidents for every driver, or that in one year roughly one in ten drivers will have an accident. And there are 0.11 accidents for every vehicle, or roughly one in ten vehicles will be involved in an accident. For an officer to be considered "average" when evaluated against the public's accident rate, for every ten drivers in your department, you should experience 1.2 accidents. Take a close look at your department's accident rate. If more than 10 percent of your vehicles are involved in accidents, you are above the average for that of the general public.

For a municipal department to be considered average, it should have no more than 23.6 accidents for every million miles its vehicles are driven. If the vehicles are driven 500,000 miles, the department should experience half that number. If driven 1.5 million miles, then multiple 1.5 × 23.6 accidents, or 35.4 accidents per million miles.

Driving Is a State of Mind

2

Police officers must be in good physical and mental condition. This is the very foundation of safe driving. Few people will ever have to drive under the stressful conditions always present in the front seat of a police cruiser. To be a standard of health befits the role of the police officer. If you suffer an injury that prevents you from operating your vehicle to its fullest capability, you should probably not drive that vehicle.

To illustrate just how important physical condition is to safe driving, consider this scenario: You have just spent five minutes rolling around on the ground with an individual measuring about 6'5" who does not feel that this is an appropriate time to be handcuffed. As a result of your brief but strenuous workout with this individual, you have developed a shoulder injury. Because of your sore shoulder, it now takes you just a little longer to move the steering wheel, say, about one second longer. You are transporting your handcuffed prisoner to the station, driving along at 40 mph, when suddenly someone ahead of you runs a stop sign. Because you are traveling at 40 mph, you are also traveling at the rate of 58.8 feet/sec. And because it now takes you a second longer to react at the wheel, you also need an additional 60 feet (more or less) to get out of the way.

These 60 feet could mean the difference between a wild story to tell the guys over coffee back at the station, or spending the next five years fighting a lawsuit.

The solution is simple: If anything makes you feel like you can't drive, *don't*. If there's any way you can avoid it, *avoid it*.

EYESIGHT

Vision is the foundation of safe driving. As a police driver, the most important aspect of your physical well-being is the quality of your eyesight. Virtually every action you take with your car is based on eyesight. You can't avoid an accident if you can't see it. You must develop a questioning attitude that heightens your awareness of both what you can and cannot see. Don't just base your driving performance on what's directly in front of you. Good drivers anticipate what can or could happen. Drivers must be prepared for what might be lurking behind corners, on the other side of hills, and moving through intersections.

The most important thing to remember is that you should be able to stop your vehicle in the distance you can see. This is especially true, and especially difficult to do, during an emergency run.

In that situation, about the best you can do is slow down as you enter an area in which your vision is impaired or restricted.

Although we use all our senses when driving, more than 90 percent of the information we need to control the vehicle comes from what we see. Driving so fast that we cannot stop in the distance we can clearly see is absolute insanity. It is simply looking for trouble.

Vision is a complex sense, affected by a number of variables, many of which we have no control over. Your vision inside the car is not only affected by physical limitations but also by such factors as tinted windshields or a convex rear or sideview mirror that can distort the image you see in that mirror. If you are about to pass another vehicle and use that convex side mirror, remember that it is not to be used as an accurate indication of where that other vehicle is in relation to your own, just that the other vehicle is there.

Complicating the issue further are factors such as fatigue and the time of day you are on patrol. For example, a routine patrol down Main Street at 2 A.M. does not tax your vision or create much stress of itself. But because of the late hour, you may be having trouble keeping your eyes open.

Conversely, traveling that same stretch of Main Street at 65 mph on a Saturday at noon places an incredible demand on your vision and on what you need to see and how quickly you need to see it. You would find this situation far more motivating and would probably have no trouble keeping your eyes open during it.

Windshields

No discussion of driving vision would be complete without examining the medium through which you are nearly always looking: the windshield. Rule 1: Never drive with a fogged windshield or side mirrors. This sounds pretty elementary, I know, yet we've all seen people driving down the road with a windshield nearly completely fogged. Usually they've managed to clear a little peephole in the windshield, but their side and rear windows are completely fogged or covered with snow. Their cars look like little tanks, with the drivers peering through their tiny slits.

As police officers, you cannot afford to indulge in such foolishness. Do not drive until you have cleared all windows and mirrors. Vision is the foundation of safe driving.

Windshield visibility. Just how much visibility do we have when looking through a windshield? A nontinted windshield permits

89 percent of the perpendicular light to pass through. Since almost no modern vehicles have perpendicular windshields (the exceptions being Jeeps and other utility vehicles), the real-world windshield value in this area is more like 83 percent of the light. What does the National Highway Transportation Safety Administration (NHTSA) have to say about this? Their rule is that the windshield needs to pass only 70 percent of the light to meet safety standards, and that is as measured through a perpendicular windshield. The result is that most windshields on commercially available cars today permit about 62 percent to 65 percent of the light to pass through.

FATIGUE

A driver can be in excellent physical condition, with the eyes of an eagle, but because humans, like all other mammals, have central nervous systems, they get tired. Because of the nature of the job, police officers are particularly susceptible to fatigue. Like everyone else, most officers don't feel that the fatigue they may be experiencing at any given time is a serious impediment to their driving ability until the fatigue has become so serious that they are in real danger.

The symptoms of fatigue are obvious. After all, everyone has had trouble keeping one's eyes open at some time. However, the early signs of fatigue are not so obvious. All of us have had the following experience: We drive a car down a route we travel every day. Nothing noteworthy happens on the drive, and at some point on the route—an intersection, a bridge, wherever—we suddenly realize that we don't really recall the drive to that spot. It's as if we suddenly materialized at that intersection or bridge. This is a strong warning that you are fatigued.

On patrol it may happen like this: You're driving and your partner spots something suspicious when you drive by a particular location. But you don't recall passing that location. That is fatigue.

Fatigue can be caused by things you did before you came to work. Coming to work after an all-night party may be a memorable experience, but if your condition is such that you have a hard time finding the door handle of the cruiser, you could wind up with an experience you'd rather forget. Coming on shift tired or hung over can literally be fatal. Don't take this to mean that you should lead a life of sainthood in your off-duty hours. Sometimes the realities of day-to-day living make it impossible to arrive at work bright-eyed and bushy-tailed. You might have been up all night with a sick child or other personal emergency. But your state of fatigue on the job should *never* be self-induced.

Mental fatigue can cause the same problems as physical fatigue. Worries over personal problems or irritation with someone on or off the job who just gave you a hard time can cause mental fatigue. Breaking up a family dispute or having marital problems yourself can leave you mentally drained. You're not unique in reacting this way. Few people can face the situations a police officer routinely faces and then just climb into a car and drive away. As an officer, you seldom get an opportunity to take a moment to unwind after a stressful situation. Duty calls and, more often than not, you're off to the next crisis. On a busy tour of duty, you may go from one confrontation to the next all night long.

Drivers can resist the effects of fatigue by simply being aware of them, knowing that they exist, and being alert to the first warning signs. The following list outlines some of the problems that driving while fatigued creates:

1. When driving at night, you may have a hard time concentrating on your driving. This is no great revelation. When we are tired, we have a hard time concentrating on anything we do.

2. When fatigued, we tend to take more risks. You may do things while fatigued you would never think of doing when well rested. Fatigue dulls the mind, especially during high-risk pursuits.

3. When tired, drivers have a tough time keeping their cars in the proper lane. They may weave and appear drunk, but they're not. They're just very, very tired. But the results are the same; it's a dangerous, accident-producing situation.

4. A fatigued driver often speeds up and slows down erratically. If you find yourself doing that, be aware of it. You're fatigued.

5. If a fatigued driver ignores these early warning signals and continues to drive, vision deteriorates and it gradually becomes very difficult to see. Attention focuses forward. The driver will begin to miss signals or signs in the peripheral vision area. In other words, the driver develops "tunnel vision." This accounts, in part, for many of the police accidents that occur near the end of a long shift.

We all know that the solution to fatigue is rest. Experiments indicate that the most successful driving is performed when rests of 20 to 30 minutes were taken for every one and a half to two hours of driving. The time-honored cure of drinking coffee to stay awake is only a stopgap, temporary measure. Sure, the caffeine can bring you up fast, but as the kidneys eliminate it from the body, it will also bring a person down—fast. The surest way to recover from fatigue is to stop and rest or take a short nap. Of course, if you're supposed to be on duty at the time, this may not go over too well with your superiors. A brief stop and just a leg-stretching short walk can be valuable in fighting fatigue.

Seating Position

There is no single clear-cut, foolproof way to beat fatigue. But seating position is often critical. The way you sit in a vehicle can help you remain alert.

Many people blame car seats for an uncomfortable ride. Most of the time the seats aren't to blame; it's the way we sit in them. Sitting erect allows us to stay alert longer. Shoulder and arm position are also important. Get in your cruiser and place your hand at the top of the steering wheel. When you do this your shoulder should not be out of contact with the seat back. If your shoulder does not rise off the seat back, you'll find that when you execute an emergency maneuver, you'll be lifted right off your seat. Instead of using the steering wheel to control the car, you'll be using it to hold yourself in place.

As you sit comfortably, look at your arms. If they are bent at the elbow more than 90 degrees, the result will be poor circulation and very tired arms in a short time.

One of the most common errors is caused by people sitting too close to the steering wheel. This can be interpreted as a lack of confidence on the part of the driver, or an indication of poor eyesight, or both. The opposite extreme—getting too relaxed behind the wheel—can also be a major problem. A driver with the window rolled down, elbow propped up on the sill, and driving with one hand is probably just a little too relaxed and overconfident for police work.

Hand Positions

Consider the steering wheel as a clock, with the top as 12 o'clock and the bottom as 6 o'clock. Your hands should be at the 3 and 9 o'clock positions. *Both hands should remain on the wheel unless it is necessary to operate another control in the car with either hand.*

'AVOID DRIVING A CAR WHILE TAKING THIS PRODUCT'

The above warning appears on the back of many over-the-counter medications. The makers of these medicines are trying to tell you something. Even something as mild as a hay fever pill can seriously impair your ability to control a vehicle. Read the label before you take *any* medication and before you drive. Of course, this means any drug, whether taken for a medical condition or for recreational purposes. As a law-enforcement official, you should never take any of the latter anyway, not if you value your career.

If taking a prescription medicine, you should ask your doctor about the effects it will have on your work. If it will affect your performance, do whatever you can to avoid driving. What happens when drugs or alcohol and driving mix is that these substances suppress the brain's ability to process information. The amount of information-processing needed to control a vehicle, for instance, simply becomes more than your newly impaired brain can handle. The drugs that do this need not be illegal; over-the-counter medications will also do nicely.

All tests examining the role of alcohol in driving impairment have indicated the same thing: that alcohol reduces the capacity of the mind to process information from both the road and the overall driving environment. Similar tests performed using marijuana showed different results. Although reaction times were slowed by marijuana, they were not slowed as much as when test subjects were given alcohol. The conclusion would seem to be that marijuana is less dangerous than alcohol when it comes to driving. Nevertheless, marijuana use is still a dangerous, foolhardy, and illegal thing to do.

What happens when driving under the influence of marijuana is what has been termed a "perceptual failure"; you simply do not see things in time to react to them. Put more bluntly, you're so stoned, you don't recognize you're in trouble until it is too late to do anything about it. For the public, the use of marijuana comes down to a matter of personal responsibility. For a police officer, smoking marijuana is more than just an individual decision. It's insanity for an officer to smoke grass. It can cost you your job, ruin your career, and, when it comes right down to it, makes you no better than the people you're arresting for doing the same thing.

THE GOOD DRIVER

A common misconception about driving is the definition of "the good driver." Just what is a "good driver"? Many people mistakenly substitute timidity for prudent caution in driving. Any racing driver will tell you that only fools take unnecessary chances. Caution is the byword of racing.

People who believe they are good drivers because they can drive fast are sadly mistaken. Simply driving fast requires little skill if one is simply driving in a straight line. Professional drag-racing drivers might differ with this evaluation, but that is a highly specialized form of straight-line driving.

Too often, people who don't know any better think they're good drivers because they:

- Pass people whenever they please, without any regard to safety.
- Try to beat a yellow light.
- Squeal tires every time they accelerate from a dead stop.
- Weave through traffic and drive with one hand.
- Cut others off in order to get ahead of them.

People who regularly do this aren't good drivers; they're idiots. Don't mistake using your head before making a move as being timid, and don't mistake fear for cowardice. Driving through city streets at 65 mph *should* put some fear into you. Sure, handling a car at high speeds can make the adrenaline flow. You may like that adrenaline high, but don't get used to it. To get it, you are putting your life and the lives of the people you are sworn to protect in a great deal of danger.

Seat Belts

The facts are in on seat belts: *They save lives.* Plain and simple. Police officers have sometimes questioned the use of seat belts, expressing fears that belts could get in the way of fast exits from the car, or that a belt could snag on a revolver, causing the gun to be yanked from the holster. While both events might occur, a little forethought should prevent them. *There is no excuse for not wearing a seat belt!*

Why do we need seat belts? It's amazing that some driving professionals ask that question when the answer is so obvious. Sure, we all know the story of someone who didn't wear a belt and was tossed free of the car in the accident when the vehicle blew up and became a fiery inferno. That individual must be the most popular person in the world because everybody knows that person. Stop and think about this story. Can you imagine what it would be like to be thrown free or jump out of a car that was moving along at 40 mph? It could ruin your whole day. Along with your face, and most of what's attached to it.

Wearing seat belts is merely a recognition of Sir Isaac Newton's laws of motion. Objects at rest tend to stay at rest; likewise, moving objects tend to keep moving. Thus, large, stationary objects such as telephone poles or trees want to stay that way. Your vehicle, traveling toward that stationary object, wants to keep moving. When the stationary object meets the moving object, something has to give. Generally, this "something" is you and your vehicle. When your car hits the pole or tree, it stops. Unfortunately, unless you are secured inside the car by a seat belt, you don't stop moving. You travel forward to meet, and sometimes go through, the windshield. Seat belts are designed to keep this from happening.

Another complaint about seat belts is that they are uncomfortable. Try wearing a neck brace or spending a few weeks or months in traction. You'll really know what discomfort is.

If the belts are uncomfortable, you're probably not wearing them properly. Belts should be worn so there is none of the slack that allows the torso to move forward before it is stopped by the belt. In a severe collision, a too-loose belt might produce bruises, but bruises are far better than having your face introduced to the windshield. The lap portion of the belt should be comfortable but tight. The buckle should never be over your stomach, but at the side, on the hip. Most cars today have inertia-reel seat belts that allow passengers and drivers freedom of movement inside the car while retaining the ability to lock in place when sudden tension, such as that encountered in a sudden stop or collision, takes place.

The only time you should not have your belt on is when you are about to make a felony stop. In this case, you want to have full freedom of movement as soon as the cruiser comes to a halt. Undo the belt just before you begin the stop. In the event of a problem, you do not want to be hung up in the belts, trying to free yourself.

Any other time, wear your belt. Where mandatory seat belt laws are in effect, automobile fatalities have gone down. That's not speculation. That's fact.

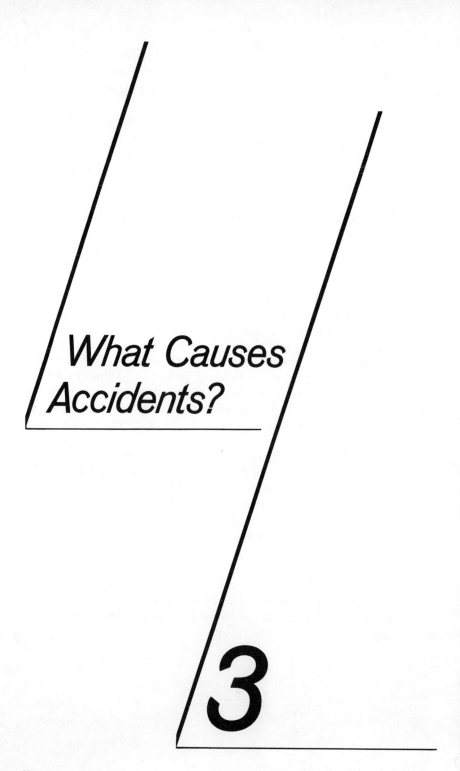

What Causes Accidents?

3

THE DRIVING SYSTEM

Your ability to avoid accidents does not depend solely on your ability to control the car. When driving a car, we're at the mercy of the environment around us, and at the mercy of the vehicle we are driving. Like Mother Nature, driving is a balance, and that balance is called the *driving system* or "driver's triangle," which is made up of three components: the *driver*, the *machine*, and the *environment* (Fig. 3-1). When an automotive accident occurs, it is caused by a failure of the driving system. Either the driver, the vehicle, or the environment failed.

The Machine

Police departments provide their officers with the safest vehicles they can afford. A little-known fact about police cruisers is that they are among the best-handling American cars made. In many instances a new police vehicle has greatly superior handling capabilities compared to expensive sports sedans made in Europe. However, no matter how well a police vehicle handles, it is only a machine, and like all machines it has its limitations. These limitations are aggravated when maintenance is poor or insufficient. But accidents caused by outright mechanical failure are relatively rare. Accidents brought about by impaired vehicle performance attributable to poor or relaxed maintenance standards are difficult, if not impossible, to compute.

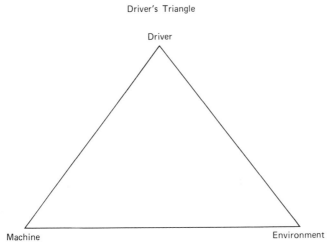

Figure 3-1   Driver's triangle (driver, machine, environment).

When new, police vehicles have excellent handling qualities. While some police departments do suffer from poor maintenance, most departments are equipped with far better vehicles than the general public.

The Environment

The United States has the best-designed and constructed highway system in the world. Nevertheless, these roads are not immune to the effects of weather and use. If the road surface has been "modified" by nature, then the driver and machine portion of the driving system must cope with these changes. In some rare instances the road conditions have deteriorated to the point that the driver/machine combination cannot compensate.

It is the environmental portion of the driving system that puts police officers at a distinct disadvantage. Because police have to drive in all sorts of weather conditions, they are much more at the mercy of the environment than is the driving public.

The Driver

The third leg of the driving system triangle is the only truly flexible, adaptable factor: the driver. The driver is responsible for the successful implementation of the driver/machine relationship. If the driving system fails, only the driver suffers. The proof lies in the numbers. About 89 percent of all vehicular accidents are caused by driver error (this figure is clouded by the fact that 48 percent of that 89 percent figure is directly attributable to accidents caused by drinking). But the remaining 41 percent were clear-headed drivers who somehow got into trouble.

DRIVING PROBLEMS

As mentioned previously, auto accidents are the fourth leading cause of death in the U.S. This gives us an idea of the size of the problem we are dealing with here. The biggest problem with driving is that we don't know what the problem is. From the numbers alone, it's obvious we're doing something wrong. Yet, most people find it difficult to acknowledge their driving deficiencies. In fact, you'd be hard-pressed to find anyone who is willing to admit that he or she has anything to learn about driving at all. Most of us attended some kind of high school driver-education program and then were tested by the local authorities. After passing our written and road tests and receiving our license to drive, all of us assumed we had become instant experts. We were wrong.

The simple fact is that we all learn to drive through experience. We become good or bad drivers through the types of driving experiences we have had. If we manage to survive these experiences, there is usually no problem.

For example, here's an experience all drivers go through: the old "there's an infamous intersection near here where all the accidents happen" experience. We all have one intersection nearby that's known far and wide as a dangerous place to drive, the sort of intersection one is just plain lucky to survive. You probably have to drive through that intersection on your routine patrols and when you do cross it, you do so with caution. Why? Because experience and local legend have taught you that this intersection is dangerous and deserves caution.

ACCIDENTS

Accidents are not always accidental. They are an unexpected event that happens by chance. Accidents are caused by breakdowns in the driving system. Through research it is possible to determine the cause of an accident. Drivers must accept that most accidents are caused by driver error. Most drivers, unfortunately, are extremely unwilling to do this. People disassociate themselves from accidents. Drivers involved in accidents talk about them as though they weren't anywhere near the vehicle when it crashed.

Consider the person who says, "My car was hit by another car that went through a stop sign." To listen to this person, you'd think that no one was in either car at the time of the collision. Cars do not go through stop signs all by themselves.

Once we accept the fact that we can actually get ourselves into an accident, and that in most cases it will either be ourselves or the other driver who is the cause of the accident, then the next important concept to understand is the type of accident we are likely to become involved in. Just how is our accident going to happen? If we know the types of driving conditions that produce the greatest number of accidents, then we can be more alert during those conditions.

The first type of accident we'll look into is the two-car collision. Ninety-six percent of all two-car collisions (except two-car fatal collisions) can be described as taking place under three separate conditions:

1. The most frequent type of two-car collision is the side collision. Out of all two-car collisions, 44.6 percent are side collisions. The most common type of two-car crash occurs when both cars are traveling in parallel courses and one crosses the path and hits the side of the other.

2. The second most frequent type of accident is the rear-end collision. Some 27.7 percent of the accidents discussed here fall into this category. This usually happens when one vehicle is stopped and the second car, overtaking from the rear in a straight line, hits the stopped car. The second most common rear-end crash involves the striking vehicle hitting a parked car.

3. The third most common two-car accident is a bit unusual. Amounting to 13.6 percent of the two-car, nonfatal accidents, this is the kind of head-on collision in which the two vehicles are not traveling straight toward each other. In this category, the most common accident scenario involves a striking vehicle making a left-hand turn and impacting a car coming the other way head on. The second most frequent type of head-on crash does involve both cars traveling in straight lines, directly at each other.

When these three categories are further subdivided into the 10 most common two-car crash situations, the breakdown looks like this:

1. Two cars traveling straight; one hits the side of the other (13.5 percent).

2. The striking vehicle traveling straight; it hits another vehicle making a left-hand turn (10.3 percent).

3. Vehicle proceeding in a straight line rear-ends a stopped vehicle (8.2 percent).

4. Vehicle traveling in a straight line hits the side of a vehicle that's just started to move (4.3 percent).

5. Hitting a parked car (4.2 percent).

6. Car out of control hits the rear of a stopped car (3.7 percent).

7. The striking vehicle, making a left turn, hits a vehicle head on (3.2 percent).

8. Two vehicles traveling straight and in opposite directions hit each other head on (3.1 percent).

9. Out-of-control vehicle hits the side of a vehicle making a left-hand turn (2.8 percent).

10. A car traveling in a straight line rear-ends a vehicle that is slowing down (2.6 percent).

Single-Car Accidents

The statistics for single-car accidents are very different from those for two-car collisions. According to the figures, in some 50 percent of all single-car accidents, the car was out of control before it hit anything or went off the road. This means that something happened to cause the driver to lose control of the vehicle.

Amazingly, in 40 percent of the single-car mishaps, the car was traveling in a straight line before leaving the road. For some reason, the drivers simply did not understand the problem or sense the crisis in time to do anything about it and just drove off the road. In these straight-crash situations, the drivers had various options of action, but instead did nothing. More than likely, the driver didn't have a clue either to what was happening or how to get out of danger.

Obviously some conditions are more conducive to single-car crashes. Most happen:

- On slippery roads
- On curves
- On 55-mph roads.

Statistics reveal that slippery conditions cause 45.8 percent of all single-car accidents, meaning that 54.2 percent of all single-car accidents take place on dry roads. Interestingly, 78.7 percent of *all* accidents happen on dry roads.

Many complex factors affect loss of control of a vehicle. Generally, however, the "no-control" situation is induced by the driver. Just what causes a no-control situation? Quite simply, the vehicle does not act in the manner to which the driver is accustomed. Usually, this happens when the driver puts too much input into the car. This can take several forms, among them:

- Turning the steering wheel too much
- Applying the brakes too hard
- Stepping on the gas pedal too hard.

A no-control situation can also be a combination of the above factors. In any of these actions, the driver has put a demand on the vehicle that it cannot accept. If the vehicle cannot accept the demands, the vehicle goes out of control.

What follows are five common types of police accident situations; they are not ranked in any particular order.

Oncoming car. Oncoming cars may cross the center line and into your intended line of travel. They can move into your line of travel while making a left turn or while passing another vehicle. Even on freeways, where most drivers consider themselves safe from oncoming hazards, cars can cross medians or even jump guardrails. The results are head-on crashes. If you see a car coming at you in what looks like it will be a head-on situation, your two options are to change speed and/or change direction. The best alternative is to slow down and turn to the right. It is far better to go off the road than to hit another vehicle head on. Of course, you must be aware of what you're turning into. If the right side of the road is occupied by kids getting off a school bus, you really don't have much choice—your only alternative is to hit the car.

Entering and merging. In these situations, cars can squeeze in on your path of travel at a slight angle from either side. Such vehicles are usually accelerating from either a standing or moving position. They may be changing lanes, or starting out from a parked position along the roadside. Entering and merging are common freeway occurrences, where cars merge from ramps and acceleration lanes.

The major problem with the merging car is when it comes equipped with a driver who acts without looking. In this, as in all driving problems, there is no simple solution for the driver who acts and then looks. The only solution to this in the entering and merging scenario is to make sure the other driver sees you. Be especially wary of drivers who pull away from parking spaces without looking. The best way to avoid this on a multilane street is to try to stay in the middle or left lanes. Otherwise, keep an eye out for parked cars with their front wheels canted in toward the street and that have their brake lights on. Drivers of these cars are probably getting ready to pull out and may be in such a hurry they don't bother to look before they move.

Ongoing, or cars ahead. Ongoing cars (that is, cars traveling in the same direction and at roughly the same speed you are) cause problems in two basic ways. The driver of the car ahead of you may suddenly stop or swerve out of the lane to avoid hitting another vehicle or object in the roadway. Either move on the other car's part can produce a collision. Give the car ahead of you enough room to maneuver. *Do not tailgate.*

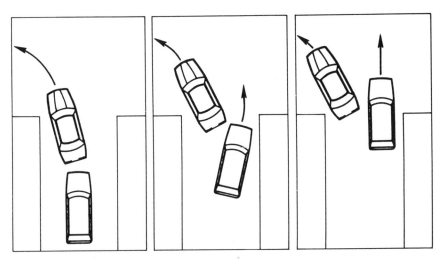

Figure 3-2 Car stopped at an intersection. The car ahead is stopped to make a left turn onto the main road. After pulling ahead somewhat, the car ahead slams on the brakes. Stop quickly if you can. If not steer to the car's right. Do not try to pass the other car; it may lead you into the path of oncoming cars that you cannot see. Drawing and caption adapted from *Medical Economics*, January 7, 1985, by permission of the Medical Economics Company, Inc.

A special situation arises when you are stopped at an intersection that has a stop sign. Here's the scenario: You are the second car in line. The car in front of you pulls out. You look left and right for opposing traffic. It looks okay and you start to pull out only to find that the driver in front of you has developed cold feet and stopped. You hit the driver from the rear (Fig. 3-2).

In this situation, patience is the key. Let the first car pull out and clear the intersection, then look both ways to see if it's safe for you to proceed.

Intersecting cars and pedestrians. Intersecting pedestrian and vehicular traffic is a source of serious problems, despite the many control devices used to regulate their interaction. Intersections are the sites for a very high percentage of all collisions. Moreover, pedestrians can come into your line of travel at almost any time.

When you pull up to an intersection, always look for conflicting traffic. *Be wary.* Even if you have the legal right of way, it doesn't protect you from the physical reality of getting hit by a car whose driver just didn't see it your way. In such a situation you will probably not have enough room or time to stop your car. Therefore, you will need to know how to swerve out of harm's way and stop as quickly as possible.

Car following.   A car following you too closely, or closing with you from behind at a high rate of speed, can crash into your vehicle's rear end should you need to stop suddenly. Tailgaters are always a serious problem, a problem made even worse at night. Fortunately, the solution to tailgaters is not too difficult—pull over and let the tailgater go by.

Accident-producing situations.   What follows are some examples of situations that police officers drive themselves into:

1. *Tailgating:* Driving too close to the vehicle in front of you. When you do this, you won't have time to react if the other driver brakes, or if there is some other type of emergency. Granted, sometimes your mission as a law-enforcement officer requires you to get close to a suspect vehicle while it is under way, whether to read a license plate, or try to check out the driver. Under such circumstances, *be careful.* Another problem: If you have your lights and siren on, or turn them on while close behind another vehicle, you may cause the driver of the vehicle ahead of you to panic and slam on the brakes.

2. *Making a sudden lane change, or a sudden change in speed:* All lane changing should be done as slowly as possible and by giving everyone around you plenty of warning that you are about to make a move. Admit it: You're often annoyed by drivers who zip from lane to lane, maneuvering about the highway as if they're the only ones on the road. So don't do the same thing yourself! Train yourself to never make a move with your car without first looking to see if someone is in the space you want to be in. And signal in plenty of time before you make that move. Nothing shakes the public's confidence in law-enforcement officers faster and more thoroughly than to see them disregard the same traffic laws they have sworn to uphold.

3. *Driving faster than traffic allows:* We'll give an in-depth analysis of high-speed driving later in this book. In certain situations, a police officer must drive faster than traffic will allow. There is very little to say that is positive about this. The law-enforcement mission demands this kind of driving from time to time, and when the time comes to drive fast, fast you must drive. Words of advice: Use your head. Drive cautiously. Don't drive yourself into a situation you can't drive yourself out of.

4. *Failure to recognize when you're in trouble:* This is one of the

toughest problems you'll face. There's not much you can do to train for this situation, because by the time you know you're in it, you may not be able to get out of it. The best thing for you to do is understand the different situations that can get you into trouble and be able to recognize them before they're inescapable.

5. *Other drivers unaware of your presence:* This can be especially troublesome when operating your vehicle during an emergency. Get those lights and siren on and keep them on. In a nonemergency, honk the horn.

6. *Not paying attention to the driving task:* Many times this is not because the driver is lazy but occurs because of drowsiness, stress, and just daydreaming behind the wheel.

7. *Driving while emotionally unstable:* Never let your emotions get ahold of you while driving. Driving while emotionally upset, especially while unusually angry or sad, can reduce your ability to recognize danger and avoid it.

VEHICLE DEFECTS

Very few accidents are caused by a defective vehicle. In modern cars, this sort of catastrophic mechanical failure is practically nonexistent. Unfortunately, while a car may be constructed quite adequately for regular civilian day-to-day driving, it might not be adequate for emergency use. Ask any police officer who teaches an emergency driving program how well the cars stand up to abnormal abuse.

Almost all vehicle defects give the driver some advance warning that a failure is imminent. Most people ignore the warning signs and keep on driving until there is a dramatic failure of the component or systems. Luckily for these people, when the component or system does finally fail, the worst thing that generally happens is that the car stops and they have to wait for a tow truck.

Tire Defects

Tires are better than ever. Today's police tires are state-of-the-art design. But like any mechanical device, it will fail if not well treated. Tire care will be covered in a separate chapter. Suffice to say that it's foolish to drive on badly worn tires.

Brakes

Don't wait until you have to toss out an anchor to stop your vehicle or until you can hear a metal-to-metal scraping when you hit the brakes. At the first sign of something unusual, have the brakes checked. Brakes will also be treated in a separate chapter.

Vision Restrictions

It is truly amazing to see the number of people who drive around with their windshields and rear windows completely covered with dirt. In order to drive, you have to see where you're going. Take the time to clean *all* your windows, and make sure the windshield wipers are in good working order.

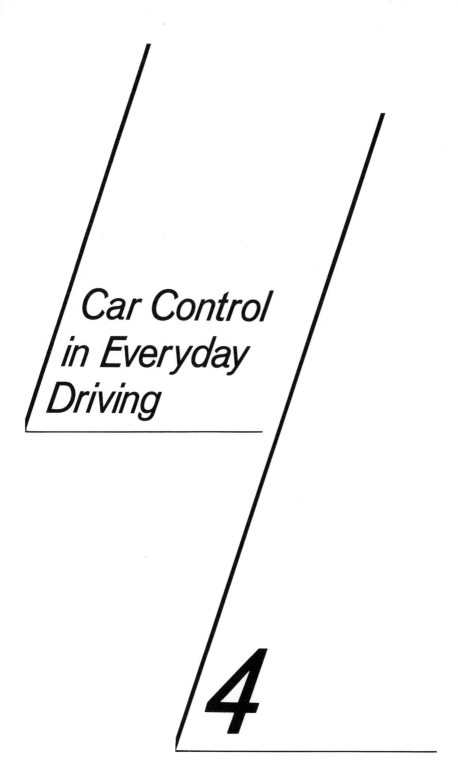

Car Control
in Everyday
Driving

4

To control cars as efficiently and effectively as possible, drivers must understand some basic principles of the science of driving. As a car is in motion down a road, the driver is managing time and space. As we drive, we measure time and space by using the car's speedometer. However, the speedometer is not the best reference possible for measuring time and space (or distance). Speedometers indicate speed, measuring it in terms of miles per hour (mph), the time it takes to cover a certain distance. It's a natural unit of reference that everyone is familiar with in driving discussions. But it's not a very useful unit of measure. Accidents do not take hours to happen; they occur in seconds, even tenths of seconds. Moreover, measuring the distances involved in terms of miles is not very useful either, because accidents happen in very small physical areas, measurable in feet and sometimes inches.

Thus, we need to rethink our frame of reference when we talk about how accidents happen. The frame of reference we'll find most valuable for this is *feet per second* (fps). Let's take a minute to see how the conversion from mph to fps works: If you are traveling at 40 miles per hour, you are traveling 58.8 feet per second (Table 4-1). To convert miles per hour to feet per second, multiply the miles per hour by 1.47. Let us now see how using feet per second as a measurement makes a big difference when discussing accident causes.

You're on routine patrol, driving along at 40 mph (or 58.8 fps). Something causes you to look away from the road for three seconds. At the same moment, another driver starts to cross an intersection 300 feet (the length of a football field) in front of you. Because your attention was diverted for three seconds and you were traveling at 58.8 fps, you drove a total of 177.4 feet without looking where you were going. This puts you 122 feet from the intersection and its conflicting traffic. At this point, you look forward again, see the other traffic, and realize you've got to do something. Can you avoid hitting that other car?

TABLE 4-1. CONVERSION FROM MILES PER HOUR
TO FEET PER SECOND

Speed (mph)	Distance (ft./sec.)
20	29.4
30	44.1
40	58.8
50	73.5
60	88.2
70	102.9

Let's examine this situation a little more closely. You're 122 feet in front of the conflicting traffic, and closing with that traffic at 58.8 fps. If you can get your foot on the brake in half a second, you're very fast. Traveling at your speed, that half-second represents about 30 feet. So at the point of applying your brakes, you are about 92 feet from the traffic, still doing 40 mph (58.8 fps). You have just applied your brakes. Can you stop in time?

At this point, avoiding a collision would depend more on luck than skill. The problem here is speed. According to the National Safety Council, excessive speed is the single largest cause of accidents. This doesn't mean just driving over the speed limit. This means going too fast for the traffic situation developing around you. Because excessive speed is so dangerous, it would behoove us to gain a better understanding of speed and how to control it.

SPEED

As a police officer, you will have plenty of opportunities to drive "fast." But how fast is fast enough, and how slow is slow?

Most of us would agree that 100 mph is fast and 20 mph is slow. But these are both relative values dependent on conditions. For anyone who has ever tried to drive on an icy road down an icy hill, toward a busy intersection, 20 mph is downright exciting.

Speed plays all kinds of tricks on us. Among the most deadly is the relationship of speed to stopping distance. Although this subject will be covered in more detail in later chapters, it will serve us well to take a quick look at the effects speed has on stopping distances. In

TABLE 4-2. HOW LONG DOES IT TAKE TO STOP A CAR?

mph	Dry (ft.)	Wet (ft.)	Snow (ft.)	Ice (ft.)
20	25	70	105	160
30	55	110	170	275
40	105	170	275	
50	188	250	410	
60	300	350		
70	455			

If you drive from a dry surface onto a wet surface, the time needed for safe stops increases dramatically. Why? Drivers will usually answer, "Because the road is slippery." And just what does that mean? It means the coefficient of friction between the road and tire is less than that needed for good, safe traction.

TABLE 4-3. EXTRA SPEED: HOW LARGE
A FACTOR IN SAVING TRAVEL TIME?

Average mph			Miles to Destination			
			5	10	20	30
30			10	20	40	60
40	Minutes	of Travel	7.5	15	30	45
50			6	12	24	36
60			5	10	20	30

If your speed is 30 mph and you need to travel 5 miles,
it will take you 10 minutes to arrive at your destination.
If your speed is 40 mph, it will take 7.5 minutes to get
there. The difference is just 2½ minutes.

Table 4-2 you will see that it takes 55 feet to stop a car traveling at
30 mph on dry pavement. If we double that speed, do we double the
stopping distance? Sadly, no. In fact, the stopping distance increases
by a factor of four. That's a good rule of thumb to remember: For
every doubling of the car's speed, it takes four times as much distance to bring the vehicle to a halt.

In a pursuit, speeds vary greatly, as can the nature and quality
of the surfaces driven on. Be aware of the effects of speed on braking
distances. The faster you go, the longer it takes. Learn this intuitively
so you don't have to think about it; you just *know* it. Misjudging or
disregarding speed can be a killer.

Take a close look at Table 4-3. Unless it's a real emergency,
driving fast merely for the sake of driving fast is not too bright.

PASSING

Head-on collisions represent a substantial number of accidents. Before you decide to pass someone, think. Ask yourself some questions: "Why am I passing this car?" "Is this maneuver absolutely
necessary?" If you want to pass someone who is slowing you down
by driving slowly themselves, then passing is justified.

But are you passing the car ahead of you because there is an actual emergency, and you have to get where you're going in a hurry,
or are you passing because your ego just can't stand to have anyone
ahead of you? Think before you make your move because if you
recklessly pass someone while driving your police cruiser, both you
and your department will suffer the consequences.

If you are in the wrong lane when your accident happens, or you force someone off the road because you were in the passing lane, it won't make any difference what the circumstances were. You may have had your overhead lights on, siren screaming, and have been in hot pursuit of Public Enemy No. 1, but you're still going to spend a lot of time in court explaining to a judge and jury just what you and your cruiser were doing in that lane.

If you must pass someone, realize and remember that you and your vehicle are going to be spending a good deal of time in the wrong lane. If you are traveling at 50 mph, passing someone going 40 mph, you will need about 10 seconds and 735 feet to safely complete the pass. If the crest of a hill is just 300 feet away, and there's a car just out of sight on the other side of that hill, you're going to have some problems on your hands—soon. When it comes to passing, consider the following cautions:

- *Never* pass on curves.
- *Never* pass at intersections.
- *Never* pass when crossing railroad tracks.
- *Never* pass at night when you can't see far ahead of you.

All these practices are hazardous to your health.

The question of whether or not to pass is never an easy one. Here are some guidelines:

1. *If there is an oncoming car, how far away is it?* Do I *really* have enough time and space?
2. *Is this pass legal?* If not, make especially sure you have enough time and space to make it. If you are involved in an accident while making an illegal pass, you're in big trouble.
3. *Is this pass really necessary?* Why are you passing this car?
4. *Is the car you are about to pass aware of your presence?* Sometimes it appears obvious that it is; after all, your lights are flashing and your siren is on. Don't assume this car is aware of your presence. Don't assume that the driver is in any condition to react rationally. Some people panic at the sight of a cruiser approaching from the rear with lights on and siren roaring. They may do something irrational, like cut in front of you as you start to pass, or slam on their brakes and cause you to rear-end them.
5. *Are there side roads ahead that may hide a car about to turn into your path?* Even if you can't see them, assume they're there. Use Murphy's Law and proceed, but with caution.

6. *How long is all this going to take?* Do you have enough time to pass and get back in your lane? Of course, it's impossible to get out a yardstick and measure the distances involved. Likewise, while the tables in this text are useful, you'd be foolish to keep this book on the seat beside you. Can you see yourself flipping pages, trying to find the proper table while in pursuit? Estimating whether or not the pass is safe requires quick thinking. You haven't got much time. Your best friend here is your own good sense and your experience as a good police driver. But if you have to make a mistake, make it on the side of too much caution rather than not enough.

7. *Check your mirrors before you pass.* Someone may be trying to do the same thing to you. Moreover, it's just good sense to check your mirrors before you make any move with your vehicle.

8. *Signal your intentions.* Don't surprise people. Signal and accelerate into the passing lane.

9. *Are you sure your vehicle has the mechanical ability to make this pass safely?* Some police cars aren't as powerful as they should be. Sometimes the luck of the draw gives you one that might be in need of a tune-up or have some other small mechanical problem that could inhibit performance. Determine whether you have the accelerating power you'll need *before* you need it.

10. *Can my vehicle stop quickly and safely if I have to make an emergency stop?*

11. *Avoid passing on roads with many intersections.* Intersections contain and often conceal surprises, such as other cars making turns or proceeding through the intersection. Watch out.

12. *Be especially wary of passing in traffic.*

INTERSECTIONS

Statistically, most accidents happen at intersections. Unfortunately, we still have to drive through them. As a police officer, you are more susceptible to intersection accidents, partly because you drive through more of them, and partly because you spend a good deal of your driving time in emergency situations.

It is at the intersection that the paths of pedestrians and vehicles cross. Even though we might drive with caution at intersections, others do not. According to statistics prepared by the National

Safety Council, 27.9 percent of all fatal urban traffic accidents occur at intersections.

Another study, this one funded by the federal government, indicated a higher incidence of intersection accidents, some 37 percent. In light of these figures, it is especially alarming that 50 percent of all police accidents take place at intersections. There are a lot of reasons for this.

Many intersections restrict visibility. To make matters worse, when you approach an intersection in an emergency situation, other drivers may not understand which direction you are approaching from or misunderstand your intentions. They may do something foolish, like drive directly into your path, or just panic, and come to a complete stop, blocking everything, oblivious to your lights, siren, and horn.

It's easy to misjudge the amount of time needed to cross an intersection. Keep in mind this process takes time, about four seconds to cross a two-lane road safely. If a car is approaching the intersection at 40 mph and that car is 180 feet away (which translates as about three seconds away from you), and you choose that moment to cross the road, you're probably going to have an accident. Two objects cannot occupy the same space at the same time, at least not in this universe (Fig. 4-1).

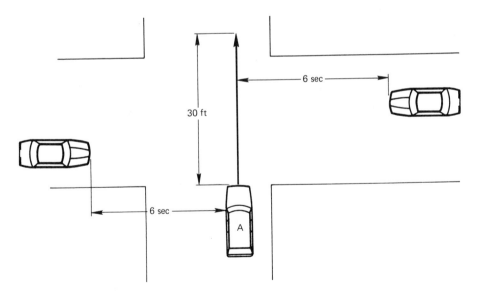

Figure 4-1   Time needed to cross an intersection.

In Figure 4-1, before crossing an intersection, car *A* must

1. make sure that from a full stop it has about four seconds to cross an intersection 30 feet wide (2 lanes)
2. check to make sure that cars approaching from either direction are six seconds from the intersection
3. look left, then right, then left again before crossing the street.

Turns are also potential causes for disaster in intersections. If you want to turn right, most cars will get you through most intersections in about six seconds, attaining a top speed of about 30 mph in that time. When beginning such a turn, make sure that any vehicles approaching from the left are at least seven or eight (or even more) seconds away (Fig. 4-2).

For example, if a car is approaching the intersection at 40 mph and is 300 feet away, it will be at the intersection in about five seconds. For you, making that seven-second left-hand turn, this scenario spells collision. *Remember:* The left-hand turn requires more time because you are crossing one or more traffic lane(s). The left-hand turn is more dangerous because in many situations it will put you into a conflicting path with oncoming cars—twice (Fig. 4-3).

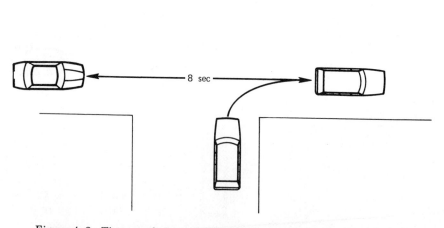

Figure 4-2 Time needed to make a right turn. From a stop it takes six seconds to turn right and accelerate to 30 mph. You should have at least eight seconds lead time before turning to the right.

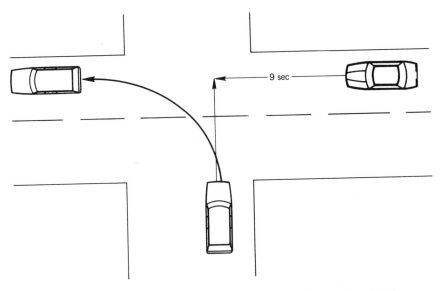

Figure 4-3 Time needed to make a left-hand turn. From a stop it takes seven seconds to turn left and accelerate to 30 mph. You should have at least nine seconds lead time before turning to the left.

When approaching an intersection under emergency conditions, supply the drivers around you with as much information as possible. Let everyone know you are there and know what you are about to do. You have a responsibility to do this. You don't want anyone to have to guess your next move. Use your overhead lights and siren. *If you are going to turn, use your turn signals.* If you have an external speaker or hailer, tell people what you want them to do. Be sure you're in the proper, legal lane to make the turn, if possible. Unless it is absolutely necessary, never make a right turn from the left lane, and vice versa. If you are about to perform a dangerous maneuver, such as a right turn from the left lane, establish eye contact with the drivers of the other vehicles involved, whether they know or don't know they are part of the maneuver. You've got to communicate your intentions because, in the event of an accident, you will be at fault.

While most police organizations have the legal right to run a red light, use good judgment before you attempt this. If you're in a pursuit, and the party being pursued just hightailed it through a red light without regard for any bystanders or other cars, that does not justify your doing the same.

TURNING AROUND AND CHANGING DIRECTION

Officers often find themselves in the awkward position of driving in one direction and then suddenly being forced to turn around quickly and take off in the opposite direction. While the so-called bootlegger turn is popular in the movies, know that there is no safe way to reverse direction.

We're going to look at three ways of changing direction. No matter what method is used, it must be done carefully. Know the legalities in your area concerning this maneuver. An illegal change in direction should be done only when there is an actual emergency. Even with an emergency, for your own safety, perform the turn in a safe area. We define a safe area as an area with good visibility.

Before attempting the turn, make sure you have a clear view of the road(s) and traffic around you. Obviously you should avoid making turns on hills, curves, and near blind intersections. The three ways to reverse direction are:

- U-turns
- Two-point turns
- Three-point turns

U-Turns

The *U-turn* is the safest of the three turns. Keep in mind that the U-turn should be legal. If it isn't, you must be in an emergency mode, with your vehicle's lights and sirens on. Although the U-turn is an easy turn to execute, you still need a lot of road and good visibility. The average police vehicle needs about 40 feet in which to turn, so you're going to need at least that much room (Fig. 4-4).

To make a proper U-turn, first stop as close to the right side of the road as possible. This gives you more room in which to execute the turn. *Look both ways* before you even begin to turn the steering wheel and start the turn. Let everyone around you know what you're going to do. Use your left-turn signal to indicate what you're planning. When you're sure everyone has been notified, turn the wheel as quickly as possible and as sharply as necessary, and complete the turn. Before pulling out and heading off in the other direction, make sure to look over your shoulder and check for oncoming traffic.

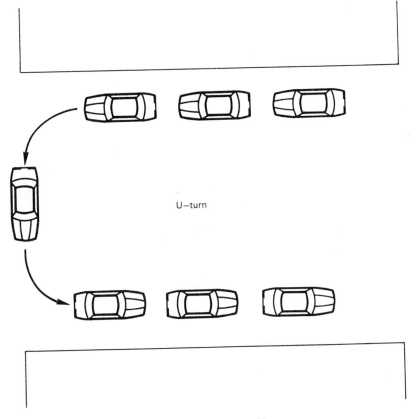

Figure 4-4 Car making a U-turn.

Two-Point Turns

A *two-point turn* means backing into a driveway, side road, or alley in order to make a 180-degree turn when the highway is too narrow, or there isn't enough visibility to make a U-turn. There are two basic ways of driving through a two-point turn: the right-hand road turn and its left-hand brother (Fig. 4-5).

The right road turn requires you to stop the car, back it into a road or driveway on the right side of the highway on which you are traveling, and then drive out onto the highway and make your turn.

The left-hand variant of this turn requires the driver to drive nose-first into a road or driveway on the left side of the road, then back onto the highway, straighten out, and drive off.

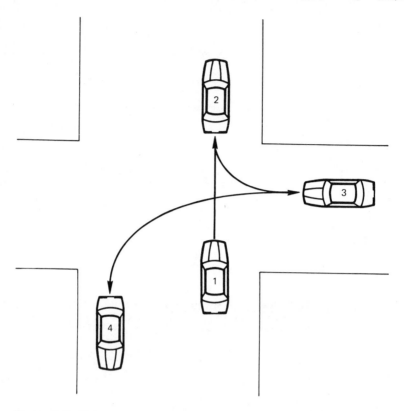

Figure 4-5 Two-point turn. These turns are made when the road is too narrow, or restricted visibility does not permit a U-turn.

The left-hand turn is much more dangerous than the right-hand turn. When you perform either of them, you will need to signal your intention to stop the car. Also, before you move backwards for the right-hand road turn, check to make sure that the path behind you is clear. Be especially watchful for pedestrians. Then back up slowly. *Remember:* It is very easy to lose control of the car while traveling in reverse. Before reentering the traffic again, make sure you can do so safely.

The left-hand road turn also requires you to signal your intention to stop, as well as your intention to make a left-hand turn onto the side road or driveway. The most dangerous moment in this turn is when you are backing into oncoming traffic. Watch out for this oncoming flow, and make sure all is clear in front of you before moving out into the traffic. Exercise due caution.

Three-Point Turn

The *three-point turn* should be made only where there is no other choice. Use this turn when the road is too narrow for a U-turn and there are no side roads or driveways that allow a two-point turn (Fig. 4-6).

To perform a three-point turn, first pull over and get as close to the right side of the road as possible, just as if you were doing a U-turn. Turn your car as though you were going to do a U-turn and follow all the standard U-turn precautions described above. Just before the front wheels of your car reach the far side of the road, turn the steering wheel to the right, check ahead and behind for oncoming traffic, put the car in reverse, and back up across both lanes.

Just prior to reaching the other side of the road, turn the wheel to the left. *Remember:* Whenever the car is moving backwards, you should be looking the same way. Drive forward. You have performed a three-point turn. It's a dangerous way of reversing direction because you are vulnerable to conflicting traffic for far too long a time. Unfortunately, sometimes there's no other way.

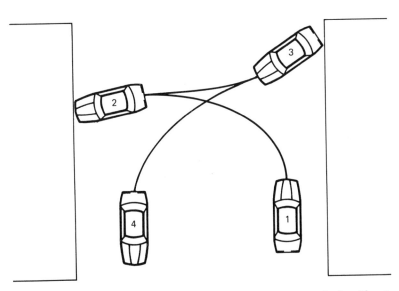

Figure 4-6 Three-point turn. Very dangerous turn-around; should not be used unless there is no other way of changing direction.

BACKING UP

Far too many police accidents happen while the car is in reverse. More often than not, these result in fender benders, not dramatic accidents, but nonetheless annoying and expensive for your department.

First of all, understand why it is difficult to back up. Cars are designed to go forward. Automobile suspensions possess a quality known as "caster." Caster is the force that helps to straighten out the front wheels after turning a corner. Caster also gives the car stability while traveling forward. Unfortunately, this stabilizing forward force destabilizes the car while it's in reverse. In other words, while driving in reverse, the steering wheel will not center automatically if you loosen your grip on it, as it will when in forward motion. Another little quirk of caster is that the car becomes unstable while traveling backwards, when small changes in steering wheel movements cause big changes in the way the car reacts to your inputs. Of course, the faster you go in reverse, the more difficult control becomes.

Highway patrol officers who may find it necessary to back up down a highway at high speed should do so only if absolutely necessary, because it is a very easy way of losing control of the car. *Remember:* The only safe way to back up is slowly. Make sure you can see where you're going. Don't try to drive fast. Use smooth applications of the brake, steering wheel, and accelerator. Keep in mind that as you maneuver backwards, the front of the car swings out to the side each time you turn and can hit someone or something. Try not to back into an intersection that contains a lot of traffic.

Admittedly, there are probably as many ways to back up as there are driving instructors. No matter what back-up technique you use, you must meet these simple goals:

- You must be able to see where you're going. It's never advisable to drive by braille.
- You must be able to reach all your car's controls. It's a little foolish to hike yourself up in the seat for good visibility, put the car into reverse, and then discover you can't reach the brake pedal.

If you are backing up to the right, look over your right shoulder. For comfort, you may put your right arm up on the back of the seat. Short people have a hard time backing up because they have a hard time seeing over the back of the front seat and out the rear window. These people have to position themselves as best they can, but they must make sure they can see out the rear window and access all the car's controls.

While this may sound a bit foolish, make sure the car has come to a complete halt before you put it in reverse. Dropping an expensive transmission out of a car by slamming it into reverse can ruin your whole day. Keep a foot on the brake while putting the car in reverse. There's nothing like shooting out of a parking space and into the path of an oncoming car to add a little spice to one's life. *Remember:* Always look where you're going.

Another problem with backing up is knowing what to do with the steering wheel. The correct direction in which to move the wheel while in reverse can be very confusing. Actually the problem is mainly perceptual. The correct way to move the wheel is really quite simple: Move the top of the steering wheel in the direction you wish the vehicle to move. It's actually no different from what you do while driving forward; it just feels different in reverse.

Here are some key points to keep in mind when backing up:

1. Never combine a great deal of steering wheel movement with a heavy foot on the gas pedal. You will surely lose control of the car.

2. Before you put the car in reverse, make sure the area in front of the car is clear. Police cruisers are often big cars, with long hoods and broad front ends. When backing up and turning in one direction, the noses of many large cars swing out to the side dramatically. Many police cruisers in America today have badly dented fenders because officers neglected to perform this check.

3. No matter how short the distance you wish to travel in reverse, look where you're going and drive slowly. Most cars feature a blind spot or spots to the rear large enough to hide a small child. Blow your horn. Give the siren a short tweek. Get out and go look for yourself. But whatever you do, be absolutely sure there is no one behind you when you back up.

4. If you are at an accident scene, or any crowd situation, let *everyone* around you know you're about to move by using your horn or siren, especially if you're about to back up.

TRAFFIC SITUATIONS

It's hard to avoid traffic, especially if you're a police officer. All of us have to drive in traffic. It's impossible to avoid, so we learn to live with it. It's a fact of life.

In heavy stop-and-go traffic, it's vital to pay attention to what's going on around us. That can be tough because, from minute to min-

Figure 4-7   Car pulling out from parking space.

ute, it may not seem like much, especially if the traffic isn't moving very fast. Keep your mind and eyes focused on the tasks in front of you. Maintain a safe distance from the vehicle in front of you. Be watchful for cars pulling out of parking spots. Many do so without looking where they are heading (Fig. 4-7).

Watch out for distracted people, the ones with the maps or the ones trying to read the directions they have been given to the local Moose hall; the ones trying to spot landmarks and otherwise relate their directions to the world around them, all the while not looking where they are going at all.

As an officer, you are going to have a lot of lost people ask you for directions. Never give directions while in traffic. Ask them to pull over and then talk to them. It's far safer than trying to hear and be heard between vehicles on a crowded street (Fig. 4-8).

When we consider the word "traffic" we often think of the heavy stop-and-go kind. But there's another kind, one that's even more deadly: high-speed traffic. This is traffic bunched together and moving very quickly. Cars are being driven quite fast, very close to one another. The main problem for officers in this situation is that when officers put on their lights and siren, the traffic suddenly looks like Moses parting the Red Sea; cars move in every direction. The problem is that some drivers look where they're going and some

Figure 4-8 Although the interaction between the police officer and the woman asking for directions is friendly enough, it is potentially hazardous. The officer should ask the driver to pull out of the flow of traffic.

don't. There's not too much you can do about this. Try not to come up fast on the car ahead of you, and give all the vehicles around you as much warning as you can.

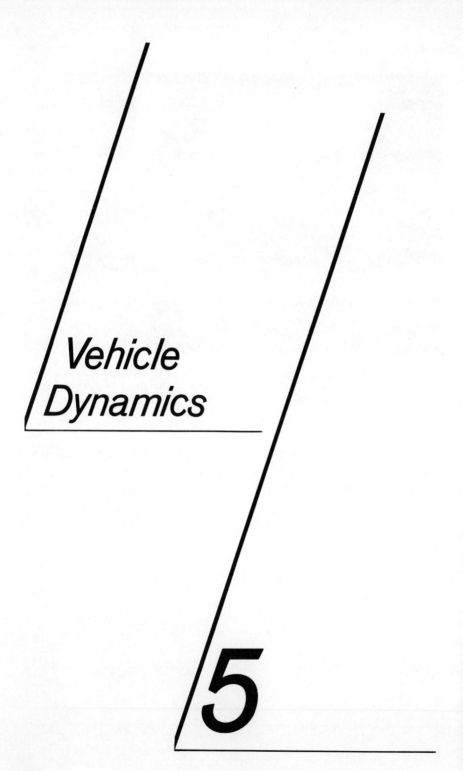

Vehicle Dynamics

5

INTRODUCTION

All of us tend to be irrationally attached to certain types of cars. whether we are law-enforcement officers or not. Some of us come from families in which everyone owns and drives Chevrolets, whereas others were raised in families where Ford may be the "officially sanctioned" car. All of us feel that some makes of cars are intrinsically better than others, but if we take a moment to think about these preferences from a rational point of view, the fact emerges that a car is simply a piece of machinery, and nothing more.

Cars can be compared to computers. A computer is an inanimate object until someone programs it. In the same way, a car is an inanimate object until someone drives it. We frequently talk about cars and computers in much the same way. We say, "The computer said such-and-such . . . ." Or "The computer made a mistake." Which is nonsense. Computers don't make mistakes; they either work or they don't. The "mistake" is made by the computer's operator. Claiming that a car "lost control" is like saying the computer made a mistake. Cars don't lose control all by themselves, except in the rare occurrence of an outright mechanical failure. It is vastly more likely for the *driver* to lose control of the car.

There are two basic definitions of this loss of control. The first isn't so much a control loss as it is just plain sloppy driving habits. All of us are guilty of sloppy driving from time to time. Remember the time you were trying to pull out of a driveway and ran over the curb? Or that time you didn't see the car that was pulling out of the parking spot and nearly hit it?

This type of loss of control really means that, although you were sitting behind the wheel, you were basically along for the ride. Loss of concentration—not paying attention—resulted in the fact that you weren't a driver; you were a passenger who just happened to be sitting behind the wheel. This is a very dangerous place for a passenger to sit.

The second type of control loss is a perfect expression of the term "loss of control." Only it is not so much the car that is out of control as the driver. In this sense, "out of control" means everything you would imagine it to be: heart pounding, eyes bulging, palms and forehead sweating, mouth going dry, stomach in a knot, and one central thought, "Oh my God, I'm going to die!" occupying center stage in your mind. At this point you have absolutely no control of either yourself or the car and that vehicle is going wherever the laws of physics take it. This is truly "out of control."

VEHICLE DYNAMICS

Anyone who spends time behind the wheel of a car, especially law-enforcement officers, needs to understand what it takes for a car to go out of control. To do this, one must have a basic understanding of *vehicle dynamics.*

Don't let the term "vehicle dynamics" scare you off. It's nothing more than a description of the physical forces acting on the vehicle. When driving, a vehicle operator can do just two things: change speed and direction. Physical forces are at work on the car that affect the driver's ability to do this. If the driver takes actions, through the car's controls, that exceed these forces, the driver will be unable to control the vehicle. Therefore, it is vital that drivers understand the forces that affect the car's ability to react to their commands. These forces are:

1. Friction created between the tires and the road.
2. Momentum and inertia built up in the vehicle while underway and at rest.
3. Centrifugal forces placed on the car when its path is altered while underway.

Of course, this is an oversimplification, but accurate enough to serve us in our discussion. First, understand the capabilities of the vehicle and exactly what happens when you move the vehicle's controls. It's very simply.

There are three ways the car can perform. It can:

1. Go (change speed)
2. Stop (change speed)
3. Turn (change direction).

Thus, a car can only do two things: change speed and direction. To expand this a little more, a car has four operating modes:

1. Forward travel at a steady speed (mode)
2. Braking (mode)
3. Accelerating (mode)
4. Turning (mode).

The most important concept to understand in vehicle dynamics is that for a car to perform the four modes of operation listed above, it must rely on adhesion between the tire and the roadway.

CONTROL

Automobiles are supported by a cushion of air contained in four flexible rubber tires. If you could place a car on a glass floor and look at it from below, you would see four patches of rubber, each a little smaller than a hand, touching the glass. These are the only points of contact between your vehicle and the road. Each of these four small patches of rubber is known as a "contact patch." They create the traction that makes the car go, stop, and turn. They are also the sources of the control feedback you receive from the vehicle (Fig. 5-1).

Although it is important to understand what makes tires develop traction, it's far more important to understand what causes cars to lose traction and to go out of control.

To control the car, rolling contact between tires and the road surface must be maintained. When the vehicle is in motion, the tires must be rolling in order to maintain control. Once the tires stop rolling and start spinning without traction or sliding outright, life gets exciting in a hurry. The reason for this sudden excitement is that two of the rolling tire patches we have been discussing are the two patches up front. These are the patches used to steer the car. If, for any reason, those tires stop rolling, we lose the ability to steer the car. Therefore, we are correct when we say:

1. The steering wheel does not steer or turn the car; it merely aims the front wheels.
2. Rolling tires both stop the car and turn the car. Front tires must be rolling in order for the car to turn. To put it in simpler terms, rolling friction is better than sliding friction. Once the tires have stopped rolling and started sliding, it is impossible to steer the car.

The four tire patches enable the car to go, or stop, or turn. In motion, tire patches have a given amount of capability for performing a given action, such as stopping. If that capability is used up, then the patch cannot do anything else—such as turn.

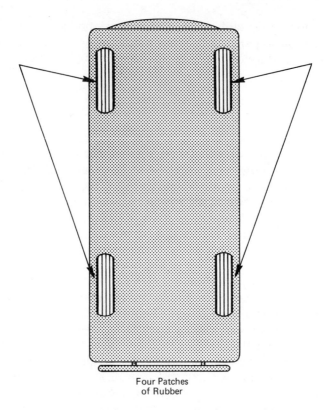

Four Patches
of Rubber

Figure 5-1   Four patches of rubber.

For example, in a front-wheel skid severe enough to stop the forward wheels from rolling (usually caused by applying the brakes too hard), the driver may suddenly find that steering the car has become impossible. No matter how much the steering wheel is turned, the car continues in a straight line. This is a front-wheel braking skid. All the available friction capability of the front tires is being used by the skid. No turning, or "cornering" force, as it's known, can develop at the front wheels. If all the front tire patches' friction capability is used trying to stop, then it becomes impossible to steer the car. The reason the car continues in a roughly straight line is due in part to simple inertia, and also the fact that the rear wheels, which continue to roll even though the front wheels are locked up, act as a sort of "rudder," keeping the car traveling forward.

Paradoxically, a front-wheel skid almost always creates the situation that drivers try hardest to avoid. Drivers slam on their brakes to stop, only to find themselves skidding right into what they were trying to avoid. How does one control such a skid? By taking the foot off the brakes, thus allowing the front tires to start rolling again, and, above all, *keeping the front wheel pointed straight.* If you have moved the steering wheel sharply to the left while skidding, then release the brakes, the car will turn, sharply and violently, in that direction.

What happens if the rear wheels stop rolling and lock up? With rear wheels locked, the car reacts violently to the slightest movement of the steering wheel, producing the maneuver known as "spinning out." How does one avoid this? Stay off both the accelerator and the brake while regaining control by means of a technique known as "countersteering," or turning the wheel in the same direction the rear end of the car swings. Because the rear end may tend to "fishtail," or swing back and forth, it may be necessary to change the direction of the wheel several times before regaining control. Throughout this procedure, keep in mind that the general idea is to keep the nose in front of the skidding wheels at all times.

LIMIT OF ADHESION

A car is a machine, and there is a limit to what it can do. We sometimes try to force a car to exceed those limits. The maximum control capacity of the tire patches referred to earlier is called the "limit of adhesion." This limit is the maximum performance available from a particular vehicle and tire design. If we try to force a vehicle to go beyond those limits, especially beyond the "limit of adhesion," the vehicle will go out of control (Fig. 5–2).

The limit of adhesion is determined by the adhesion, or grip, of the tires to the road. The maximum amount of acceleration, braking, and cornering forces possible with a given set of tires are all determined by this tire-to-road grip.

It is vital for you to understand the interrelationships between acceleration, braking, and cornering forces. The ways in which these forces interact are some of the most important concepts in driving.

In later chapters we will discuss how to drive yourself out of trouble by concentrating on the fact that the foundation of trouble-free driving is the relationship between these three forces as represented by the brake, gas pedal, and the steering wheel. How much you can move the steering wheel before losing adhesion is determined by how hard you have applied the brakes at the time. The

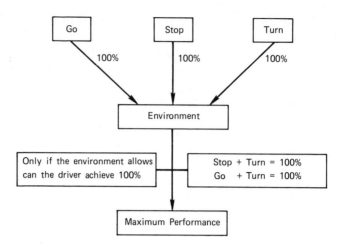

1. There can only be 100% performance from the vehicle if the environment allows it.
2. If the driver uses 100% to stop, the car will not turn.
3. If the driver uses 100% to turn, the car will not stop.
4. If the driver uses 60% to stop, he can use 40% to turn.
5. If the driver tries to use more than 100% by applying too much braking and too much steering, the driver will lose control of the vehicle.
6. This all assumes that the environment allows the driver to use 100%. If the environment only allows 50%, then the driver will be able to use only 50% of the vehicle's capability.

Figure 5-2 Maximum performance available from a vehicle.

opposite is also true; how hard you can press the brakes is determined by how much steering force has been applied.

Weight Transfer

Weight-transfer problems develop when a driver applies too much steering and braking force, or too much power and too much steering. The result in both cases is excessive weight transfer to the tires, which, in turn, puts too much pressure on the tire patch. Too much weight on the tire patch causes the driver to lose control.

As the steering wheel is turned, a force pushes on the car's center of gravity. If this force is greater than the force that the car can accept, the vehicle can go out of control. If this force produces stresses on the tires greater than the tires can accept, the tires reach their limit of adhesion and let go. Again, the vehicle is out of control.

What determines the limit of adhesion? The following factors:

1. The vertical force placed on the tire.
2. Tire design.
3. Condition and type of road surface.
4. Vehicle speed.
5. Amount of turning force.

Situation 1. The driver (see box 1 of Fig. 5-3) presses down on the gas pedal (box 2 of Fig. 5-3). If we could place a scale under the front and back wheels of the car when the gas pedal is depressed, we would see that the weight on the rear scale (A in Fig. 5-3) in-

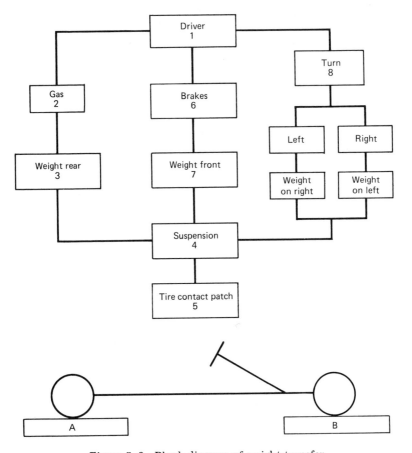

Figure 5-3 Block diagram of weight transfer.

creases, and the weight on the front scale (B in Fig. 5-3) decreases. In acceleration, weight was transferred from the front to the rear of the car (box 3 of Fig. 5-3). This additional weight in the rear presses down on the car's suspension, affecting tire contact in the rear. If too much weight is applied, the rear tires will spin.

Situation 2.   Once more, the car is on our imaginary scales. The driver (box 1 of Fig. 5-3) applies the brake (box 6), shifting weight onto the front end of the car (box 7). This time, the front-end weight increases and the rear-end weight decreases. In this case, if too much weight is shifted forward, the front tires will lock up and steering control will be lost.

Situation 3.   With the car under way, the driver turns the steering wheel (box 8 of Fig. 5-3). If the wheel is moved to the right, weight is transferred to the left—once more, by way of the suspension—and onto the tire contact patch. From the illustrations provided in Figure 5-3 we can see that a car often becomes a weight-transfer machine. When a control is moved so that the path in which the vehicle is moving is altered, or if the vehicle speeds up or slows down, then weight is moved from front to rear or from side to side. Any of these actions can exceed the tires' limit of adhesion, causing loss of control of the vehicle.

The characteristics of weight transfer onto the suspension and how those transfers affect the limit of adhesion are major factors in determining just how the car feels to the driver.

THE FEEL OF THE CAR

Many people believe that driving a car should feel like sitting on one's living room sofa. Operating their car's controls should not disturb their comfort in any way.

People who feel this way purchase the vast majority of the automobiles built every year in this country; thus, auto manufacturers go to great lengths to abolish car "feel." The end product is a vehicle for people who are missing nearly all of the experience of driving.

The irony of this is that it's possible and even desirable to feel the control limits of a car long before those limits are exceeded. Feeling the limits is desirable because this permits careful drivers more control and affords them a better idea of what is happening in the vehicle they are driving. Cars communicate to their drivers in two basic ways: *ride* and *handling*. These two very distinct sensations are often confused with each other.

Ride

Ride is the vertical motion of the wheels and tires as they rise and fall over irregularities in the road surface. Auto design engineers try to dampen this motion as much as possible by isolating it from the car's frame through the use of shock absorbers and other attenuating devices. If a lot of this motion is felt in the car's body and passenger compartment, the result is a hard-riding and frequently uncomfortable car. Ride is a comfort factor, one that can be hard or soft. A soft-riding car smooths out the bumps on the road. In this type of vehicle, a passenger could be drinking a cup of coffee as the car passes over a railroad crossing and not spill a drop. In a hard-riding car, the same passenger would end up wearing that cup of coffee.

Many people mistakenly confuse ride with comfort. A car that smooths out all the bumps of the road might be very comfortable but not necessarily a good car for police officers.

Handling

What is *handling?* Handling is the car's ability to remain in control when cornering or being driven through evasive maneuvers. It is also a complicated quality involving the entire driving system. Handling depends on the machine and the environment; it centers on the fact that a car is, at all times, a compromise between many factors. Although it is hard to define handling precisely, it is easy to make qualitative judgments as to what is good handling and what is bad handling.

In a study conducted by West German automaker Daimler Benz, researchers evaluated the current state of automotive handling technology. They came up with a compromise judgment as to just what can be regarded as satisfactory handling qualities.

First, the vehicle should respond quickly, but not skittishly or in a nervous way, to control inputs. Small movements of the steering wheel should not produce disproportionately large movements of the vehicle. This response, moreover, should be largely independent of vehicle speed.

Secondly, the vehicle should follow normal steering inputs correctly and without need of further correction. Additionally, it should be possible for large lateral (sideways) movements of the vehicle to be corrected with uncomplicated steering motions.

Thirdly, alternating quick releases of throttle and subsequent brakings should produce no unexpected and/or dangerous side movements of the vehicle.

Finally, under varying road irregularities between the left and right sides of the car, and in crosswind conditions, the driver must be able to maintain a straight course easily.

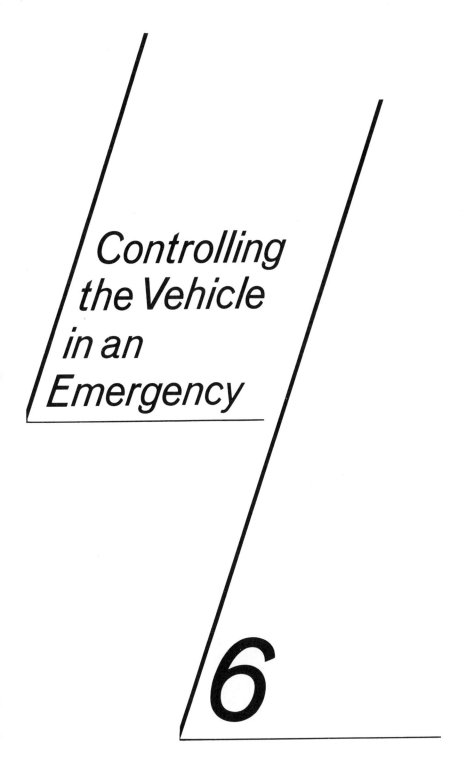

Controlling the Vehicle in an Emergency

6

Police officers are far more likely to drive into emergency situations than are everyday drivers. Unexpected situations demand immediate action. When driving a police cruiser in an emergency, unexpected situations can happen at any time.

In a previous chapter we discussed the locations where accidents are most likely to occur. Now we'll take a look at the reasons behind emergency situations. Emergencies often happen because the driver:

1. Did not have enough time and/or distance to avoid the accident.
2. Had sufficient time and/or distance but did not operate the vehicle's controls properly.
3. Was driving unconsciously.

A study conducted for the Society of Automotive Engineers by Bio-Technology (Warrandale, Pa., paper #770801) indicated that in 44.7 percent of all accidents, the driver did not perceive the danger in time. This means that in 55 percent of all accidents, the drivers involved could have done something to avoid the mishap, but either did nothing or operated the controls of the vehicle improperly, thus driving themselves into accidents.

G-FORCES AT WORK

If an accident situation presents the driver with enough time and/or distance to safely avoid the mishap but the accident still takes place, then either the driver was unaware of the danger or the operational limits of the vehicle were exceeded and the vehicle was uncontrollable. Because it is vital to stay in control of the vehicle, we need to understand the dynamics of a vehicle involved in an emergency maneuver.

The best way to understand the dynamics of a specific vehicle is to understand how G-forces affect the vehicle's handling. Let's start by examining what happens in an emergency. Anytime the steering wheel is moved while the car is in motion, a lateral or sideways force is created—a force that pushes in the opposite direction from the direction the car is turning. This force is an expression of inertia, or, as stated in Newton's first law of motion: A body at rest tends to remain at rest, unless an outside force is applied to it, and a body at motion tends to remain in motion, unless an outside force, such as the turn of a steering wheel, is applied to it.

A small change in the G-force (or simply G) can make a very big difference in the way a vehicle handles. If the path of a 4,000-lb car is altered in a way that produces a single G, that G-force is the equivalent to 4,000 lb of force. Thus, 4000 lb are pushing the car away from its desired path.

The equation for figuring this force is a simple one: The amount of force imparted to the car equals Gs times the weight of the vehicle. If we turned our 4,000-lb car in such a way that 0.7 G was created, then we would have created 2,800 lb of force or 4,000 × 0.7 = 2,800 lb. If the car weighed 3,000 lb and was turned the same way, the equation would read 3,000 lb × 0.7 = 2,100 lb, and so forth. Understand that the lateral G-forces created in a turn are based upon both the vehicle's weight and the degree, or sharpness, of the turn (Fig. 6-1).

The reason we use G-forces as a unit of measurement is because merely saying "there are 2,800 lb of force being exerted on the car" doesn't really tell us very much. The figure is meaningless unless the weight of the car is also known. For instance, if 4,000 lb of force are exerted on a 5,000-lb car, that's no big deal. But if you take a corner in such a way that 4,000 lb are being exerted on a 2,000-lb car, you're in big trouble.

It's far easier to say, "This vehicle design can absorb 0.7 Gs." If we use our 5,000-lb car for this example, then 0.7 Gs means the vehicle can absorb 3,500 lb of force before becoming unstable. If we use our lightweight 2,000-lb car, then those same 0.7 Gs are the equivalent of 1,400 lb of force.

If you're interested in how many Gs various car designs can take, pick up some of the automotive magazines available on any

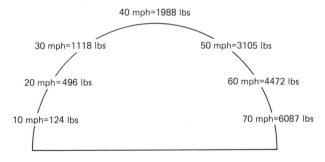

Figure 6-1 Relationship of speed to lateral acceleration. A 4,000-lb car turns the same corner at varying speeds. At 10 mph there is 124 lb of force on the car; at 40 mph there is 1,988 lb of force on the car.

newsstand. In them you'll find reviews of various cars that include road tests and the G-force ratings that resulted from those tests. Here are a few of the maximum G-force ratings of some of the cars we all know and love:

Chevrolet Corvette	0.892 Gs
Ford Mustang SVO	0.825 Gs
Saab 900 Turbo	0.774 Gs
Chrysler Le Baron	0.800 Gs
Police Cruiser	0.850 Gs

Surprised to see that your average, run-of-the-mill police cruiser can absorb a great deal of force? Police cars are designed and built to be machines with superior handling characteristics.

Thus, as we have seen, various cars are designed to absorb a certain amount of G-force. The amount of G-force exerted on a car is a function of both the degree of sharpness of the turn *and* the speed at which the car is traveling during the turn. If this G-force limit is exceeded, the result is loss of control. A car is merely a machine; if we try to use that machine in such a way that its design limits are exceeded, then this machine, like any other machine, will not work.

DRIVING EQUATION

In addition to inertia, another physical force comes into play when the steering wheel of a moving car is turned. This force is known as *centrifugal force*. When we move the steering wheel to maneuver around a corner or to avoid an obstacle, the vehicle tries to follow the path dictated by the front wheels. I said *tries*. At this point, centrifugal force is pushing the car outward, away from the direction of the turn. The concept of centrifugal force can be expressed in the *driving equation:*

$$LA = V^2/R32.2$$

where   LA = Lateral Acceleration

V = Speed of the object in motion (in this case, a car) in feet per second

R = Radius; distance of the radius travelled by the car in feet

32.2 = Force of gravity (this is a gravitational constant)

A word about equations. Equations are engineers' ways of confusing us mortals. They are also a useful shorthand way of expressing complicated concepts. It's not as important for you to understand the above equation as it is for you to know intuitively its consequences.

According to the National Safety Council, 33.5 percent of fatal accidents are caused by excessive speed. If you must make an emergency maneuver, the above equation can show us how critical speed is in determining whether or not you will suffer an accident. Quite simply, the equation shows how speed affects the maneuverability of a vehicle. Through use of the driving equation, we can see how dangerous just a small increase in speed can be.

First, let's review the equation:

LA—This is the lateral acceleration; the amount of G-force exerted on the car.

V—How fast the car is traveling in feet per second (fps).

R—The radius of the turn, roughly equivalent to the degree of sharpness of the turn, or the amount the steering wheel is turned.

What this equation tells us is that the amount of force imparted to the car is determined by how fast we're driving and how sharp we would like to turn, which is another way of saying how much we move the wheel. An average street corner has a 55-foot radius. If we take that corner at a speed no one would think unreasonable, say, 20 mph, this is what the equation tells us.

V = 20 mph or 29.4 ft/sec.

R = 55 ft

$$LA = V^2/R32.2 = \frac{(29.4)^2}{(55)(32.2)} = \frac{864.36}{1771}$$

LA = 0.49

If the car weighed 4,000 lb, such a turn would result in a force of 4,000 lb × 1,960 lb pushing the car sideward. If that car was a police cruiser capable of absorbing 0.8 Gs, its driver would have no difficulty making the turn.

If we double the speed to 40 mph, will there be twice as much force exerted on the car? Plugging these numbers into the equation gives us:

$V = 40$ mph or 58.8 ft/sec.

$R = 55$ ft

$$LA = V^2/R32.2 = \frac{(58.8)^2}{(55)(32.2)} = \frac{3457}{1771} = 1.95$$

With the same 4,000-lb car, we have increased the amount of lateral force to (4,000 × 1.95 = 7,808) or approximately *four times* the force encountered at 20 mph! It doesn't require a Ph.D. in mathematics to figure out that if you tried to exert 7,808 lb of force on a 4,000-lb car, that force is more than sufficient to push that vehicle into the "Twilight Zone," or at least off the road.

So what is the solution? (Drivers are always looking for magic answers to this one.) Guess what? There isn't one! Why did the driver lose control? *Because the driver was going too fast!*

Further study of this question produces more startling observations. A speedometer is a linear device. This means it progresses in equal steps; the space between 0 and 20 mph is the same as the space between 20 mph and 40 mph. However, the amount of force exerted on the car is not linear. Instead, it increases according to the square of the speed. Technically speaking, it is a geometric, rather than arithmetic, progression.

In other words, when a driver increases vehicle speed by a factor of *two*, the amount of force exerted on the vehicle goes up by a factor of *four*. Therefore, under the correct condition, a small change in speed can easily produce far more force than the car was designed to accept. (Refer back to Fig. 6-1.)

Example 1

We can now mathematically drive a car through an evasive maneuver. Our hypothetical car is equipped with tires capable of absorbing 1,500 lb of vertical force. At this point, tires will lose adhesion (this factor will be covered in greater depth in another chapter). Our speed is 30 mph, which, multiplied by the conversion factor of 1.47, works out to 44 ft/sec. Our hypothetical day is a clear, sunny one, road conditions are excellent, and our tires have a good grip on the road.

Suddenly, a child on a bicycle appears 90 feet in front of us. It takes you half a second to get your foot to the brake pedal, meaning you have consumed 22 feet just getting your foot in position to apply the brakes. You now have 68 feet left before your car will strike the child.

You panic and smash down hard on the brake. By doing so you have transferred excess weight from the back end to the front end of the vehicle. The weight transferred is more than the 1,500 lb the tires are designed to accept. This causes the front tires to slide, for they have passed their limit of adhesion. And because you use the front tires to steer, you've also lost directional control of the car. Therefore, you cannot steer away from the child.

Sadly, this mathematical scenario ends in hypothetical tragedy. To prevent this make-believe calamity from becoming real, use your car's maximum capabilities by always using the correct amounts of steering and braking.

Example 2

You're driving our mathematical model car again, leaving a major highway, and entering the exit ramp at a speed of 25 mph. Remember: Our imaginary car has tires with a 1,500-lb adhesion limit.

By turning onto the exit ramp you have placed 1,400 lb of force on your tires. This is fine, for the tires can handle this, *unless* you have to apply the brakes or increase the angle of your turn. By doing so, you will create more force on the tires, exceed their adhesion limits, and lose control of the car.

If your vehicle has tires capable of accepting 1,500 lb of vertical load, it can accept that load from braking, accelerating, or turning it. It can take 1,500 lb *and no more.* If you use all 1,500 lb, then when you try to turn or brake you will reach the tires' adhesion limit and the tires will let go their grip on the pavement and you will lose control.

SENSATIONS

Anytime a vehicle is in motion and we move the steering wheel, we create centrifugal forces that push the car away from the desired direction of travel. The amount of these forces depends on how fast we are going and how much we turn the wheel.

When this happens, the car starts talking to you. Not like one of the modern, computerized cars that reminds you to fasten your safety belt or that your windshield washer fluid level is low, but in the "seat of the pants" way with which pilots are familiar. Quite simply, the car communicates with you by way of its reaction to what you have done with the controls. It does this in one of three ways:

- Understeer
- Oversteer
- Neutral Steer

Understeer

By looking at Figure 6-2 we can gain a better understanding of *understeer*. The driver at Position 1 moves the wheel to allow the car to enter the corner. The driver aims the car at Point A. But instead of arriving at Point A, the car goes to Point B. This is the phenomenon of understeer.

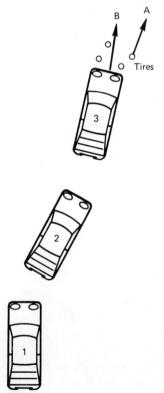

Figure 6-2 Explanation of understeer.

A look at the vehicular dynamics involved here reveals that when the driver moved the wheel to drive to Point A, the driver created a side force (lateral acceleration) pushing on the car's center of gravity. In turning, the driver creates 3,000 lb of force pushing on the vehicle. To keep the car from sliding off the road, there must be a force of 3,000 lb pushing back or the car will slide off the road. The 3,000 lb of resisting force is created by the tire contact patches.

Picture the process as though the turn produces 3,000 lb of force pushing on the middle of the car, and the tires, at front and rear of the vehicle, pushing back with 1,500 lb of force each. In this case, the car is balanced.

If, for some reason, the front tires can only provide 1,200 lb of resisting force and the rear tires provide 1,500 lb, the result will be a sensation that suggests the front end of the car is not going where the driver would like it to. This is understeer.

Understeer, then, is the interrelationship of the front and rear ends of the car. In understeer, the front wheels have less traction than the rear wheels. Among the reasons that a car will understeer are:

- Low front tire pressure.
- Uneven front tire pressure. Sometimes a car will understeer in one direction and not in another. This is because one tire has lower pressure than the other.
- Bald tires in the front.
- Mismatched tires: radials in the back and bias-ply tires on the front. The front of the car will push out—that is, resist the turn. In racing this is known as *pushing, plowing,* or understeer.

The above explanation is an oversimplification of what actually takes place, but only because it's rather complicated to explain the specifics of the vehicle dynamics involved. However, it is interesting to know that most automobiles built in the U.S. are designed to produce understeer. American engineers feel it's safer.

If understeer does occur, your objective should be to get some of the vehicle's weight onto the front tires. This will make the front tires grab the pavement more securely and start turning the vehicle. Sometimes just taking your foot off the gas will transfer enough weight forward to do the job. In some cases, it may be necessary to apply the brakes in order to increase the weight transfer to the front wheels. If this is done, great care must be taken not to overcontrol the car and throw the vehicle into a state of oversteer.

Oversteer

Oversteer is the opposite of understeer. In going around a corner, the vehicle is aimed at Point A (Fig. 6-3), but the vehicle instead ends up at Point B. In oversteering, the car develops the same seesaw motion as that encountered in understeering, except that in this case it's the rear tires that are providing the lighter amount of traction and the front tires that are loaded so that they adhere to the pavement better. The result is that the rear end of the car loses traction first, so that the rear begins to move toward the outside of the turn. This "fishtail" effect may be caused by a sudden application or withdrawal of power during a turn or by a sudden movement of the steering wheel during a turn. Moreover, oversteer can be created by any of the causes of understeer mentioned above, with the exception that in oversteer it is the rear tires, not the front, that are the critical element. Low rear tire pressure causes oversteer.

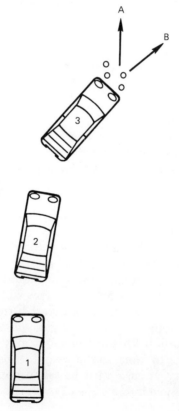

Figure 6-3 Explanation of oversteer.

To overcome oversteer, turn the front wheels to the outside of the turn. That is, turn them in the direction that the rear wheels are attempting to move. Use the accelerator so that power is applied to the rear wheels, which will force the car toward the inside of the turn and regain control. Applying power at this moment is tricky; too much power can spin the vehicle in the opposite direction.

How many accidents can be attributed to understeering or oversteering? In a study conducted by the Society of Automotive Engineers, results indicated that as the tendency for automobile understeer design increases, the accident rate decreases. A car with a high value of initial understeer will tend to wander when traveling down a straight road and be relatively insensitive to minor steering inputs. This handling quality could be important in situations in which the driver's attention is momentarily distracted from the road.

Caution: A quick shift from understeer to oversteer is very dangerous. If a car does this, check for tire intermix: that is, the mismatching of bias-ply tires and radials on the same vehicle. Cars must have one or the other type of tire *on all four wheels.*

SKIDDING

So far we've been discussing some of the gentler forms of control loss. Let's move on to the "Oh my God!" kind of situations and learn what to do about them.

When you lose control of the car, you have entered a skid situation, and not all skids are created equal. Skids are caused when the driver applies more input to the vehicle than the vehicle design can take. Of course, the amount of input a given design can handle is affected by the weather, road conditions, and other environmental factors, but essentially it was the driver who goofed by applying too much input on brakes, the accelerator, or steering wheel. Skids have their own characteristics, which we shall now discuss.

Four-Wheel Skid

A four-wheel skid results when the driver tries to shove the brake pedal through the floorboards. This unusually hard application of the brakes locks up those wheels, which cease to rotate. In such a skid, the path of the car is not predictable. Unfortunately, many drivers in a four-wheel skid don't immediately think they're in this kind of skid because they don't feel they hit the brakes hard enough to produce a skid.

There's only one solution to this problem: Take your foot off the brake pedal—*now!* You must get those wheels rolling again. Once the front tires are rolling, control is returned to the driver, who may then be able to steer out of trouble. If the present danger requires some additional braking, this must be done gently, with less pressure than before, or this whole dangerous chain of events will repeat itself.

Excessive acceleration causes what is known as a "power skid." This occurs almost exclusively on rear-wheel-drive cars. Most power skids happen when roads are slippery. They're caused by too much power going to the rear wheels. The tire/road combination cannot accept that much power, and the tire begins to spin. In a power skid (we're talking about rear-wheel-drive cars here) the back end of the car will swing out, in some instances spinning the vehicle in a complete 360-degree spin. This maneuver is probably familiar to anyone who has ever driven on ice. Once more, the solution to the power skid is to ease your foot off the accelerator until the wheels stop spinning, and only then make any necessary steering corrections.

The Front-Wheel-Drive Power Skid

Although not many police departments use front-wheel-drive cars today, they are the wave of the future and it won't be long before we'll all be driving them. The power skid is handled differently in a front-wheel-drive car. Front-wheel-drive means the front wheels are the wheels accepting power from the engine; thus, in a power skid, those are the wheels that are spinning. Once again, this type of skid generally takes place on slippery surfaces, and the best way out of it is to take your foot off the gas pedal and try to steer out of the skid without using the brakes. If needed, apply brakes *very* sparingly.

A cornering skid takes place when a driver enters a turn too fast and too sharply. This causes the rear end of the car to swing out. The best thing to do in this situation is to ease off the gas pedal and avoid braking. When you ease off, you'll find the car's rear end will begin to track in its original position again.

REACTION TIME/SENSE OF TIMING

Many factors can affect your reaction time. Before we talk about them, let's find out just what reaction time is. Reaction is the sum of the time needed for:

1. The brain to receive information from the senses. The senses we're referring to also include sensations of motion and related "seat of the pants" sensations.

2. Making decisions on what to do next. Many times, this is a reflexive reaction that carries a potential for danger with it, such as immediately smashing down on the brake pedal when we feel the car begin to skid.

3. Transmission of the messages from the brain to the muscles needed to react and move the controls.

4. The muscles to respond.

The most critical portion of the reaction process is step 2. After the senses detect the danger, a decision has to be made about what to do with the received information. The challenges and dangers faced by racing drivers is a good example of this process.

Many racing drivers are middle aged. Their reflexes may not be quite what they were when they were younger, but the decisions they make in the course of a race are the right ones. These decisions are based on their years of experience behind the wheel. Knowledge gained through experience often becomes intuitive so that it becomes part of our reflex reaction. Experienced pilots often gain this sort of reflexive knowledge.

As an example, let's set up a hypothetical situation with two drivers, one young, the other much older (Fig. 6-4). They are both driving toward the same intersection from the same direction. Ahead of them, a truck runs a stop sign and illegally enters the intersection so as to block the path of both drivers' cars. The younger driver applies the brake before the older driver but smashes the brake pedal to the floor and locks up both front wheels, enters an uncontrollable skid, and crashes into the truck.

The older driver, who takes more time to react, brakes carefully, applies the proper amount of brake force and steering control, and avoids the collision. The younger driver won the race to the brake pedal but lost the battle with the truck. Without intuitive experience, the quickest decision can easily be the wrong decision.

Many factors other than age affect reaction time. Reaction times can vary greatly between drivers of the same age group. Reaction times can vary according to the time of day, as much as four-tenths of a second in the morning to as much as a full second when fatigued at day's end. Four-tenths of a second may not sound like much, but at 60 mph, a driver travels 35 feet in that amount of time. That could make a life-and-death difference in an accident situation.

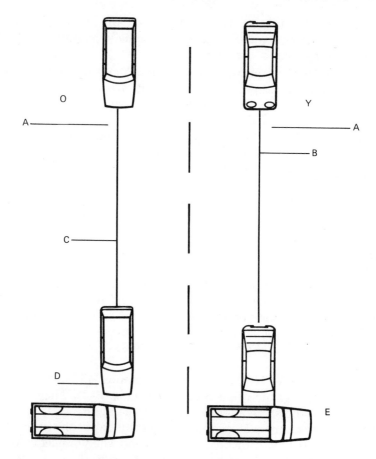

Car "Y" driven by young man.

Car "O" driven by older gentleman.

At point A both see emergency.

Car "Y" reaction time to get his foot to the brake is 0.5 sec., which will use up 45 feet. Point B.

Car "O" reaction time to the brake is 1 sec., which will use up 90 feet. Point C.

Car "Y" driver has slammed on the brake, locking up both wheels. The car enters an uncontrollable skid, lasting 1.5 seconds or 135 feet. Point E.

Car "O" takes 0.5 sec. to make a decision; he travels 45 feet. Point D.

Figure 6-4   Reflexes vs. decision making.

Reaction times among tired or ill drivers can be as long as two full seconds. Again, at 60 mph, that means a driver will cover 123 feet before reacting to a threat.

The standard reaction time for a healthy person is 0.66 sec (Fig. 6-5).

After an accident, some people might ask, "Why did the driver plow into the other car when there were so many other options available?" The answer could simply be that the driver could not reach a decision before it was too late. The time required by the brain for a simple decision depends on how complex that decision is. A simple decision, such as a reflex action, can be reached in three-tenths of a second. If the problem faced by the brain is sufficiently complex to require some thought, that decision can take as long as five-tenths to two full seconds, depending on the available options and the capabilities of the individual.

The most important lesson to be learned about reaction time is that we now know not to depend on it to get us out of trouble. The classic example of overdependence on reaction time is encountered in the tailgater.

We have all been plagued by this kind of driver. The *tailgater* is someone who drives too fast and too close behind us. An emergency can quickly develop with no way for someone following that closely to have adequate time and enough room to react. The tailgater is going to plow into you if you have to stop quickly; that's for sure.

If you were to pull tailgaters over and ask them why they follow so closely, you might encounter people who honestly don't

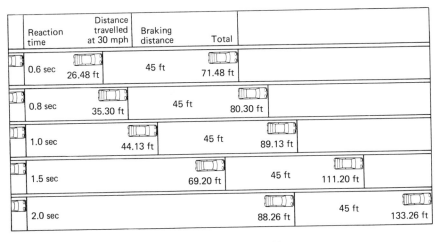

Reaction time	Distance travelled at 30 mph	Braking distance	Total	
0.6 sec	26.48 ft	45 ft	71.48 ft	
0.8 sec	35.30 ft	45 ft	80.30 ft	
1.0 sec	44.13 ft	45 ft	89.13 ft	
1.5 sec	69.20 ft	45 ft	111.20 ft	
2.0 sec		88.26 ft	45 ft	133.26 ft

Figure 6-5   Reaction time diagram.

know what you're talking about, people who really don't consider what they are doing as something dangerous, or, more disturbingly, people who think they are superdrivers who can react to anything, who can handle any driving emergency. Both attitudes are idiotic.

Can Reaction Time Be Improved?

Training can improve reaction time. Although it cannot make muscles move faster, training can cut the time required in reaching a decision. Through training, a driver can experience situations simulating driving emergencies. This helps build the decision-making process and encourages the driver to focus attention on the proper course of action in a given emergency situation. It also helps drivers stay aware of their own limitations and that of their vehicles.

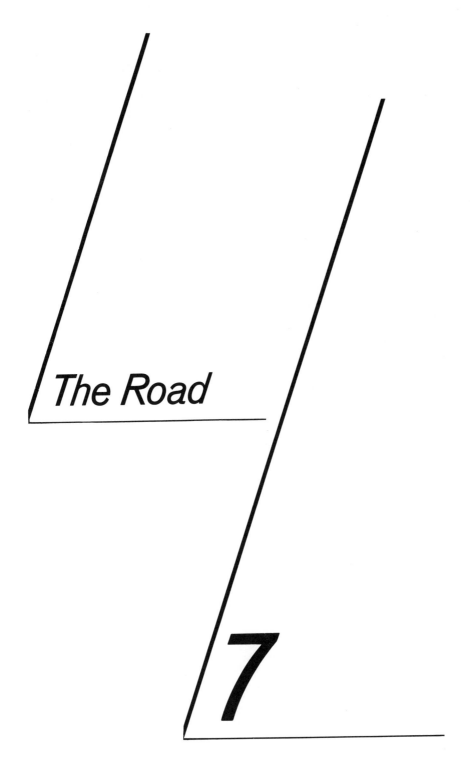

The Road

7

In automobile Utopia, all the roads are the same width, all corners the same angle. The road surfaces are all the same, all uniformly wonderful and smooth as silk. There are no hills, no valleys, and drivers seldom have to even move the steering wheel because the roads are so incredibly straight.

Unfortunately, this automotive paradise does not exist, and we do need to do things like turn steering wheels and brake and accelerate. And we have to drive around corners. As far as drivers are concerned, there are three types of corners: constant radius, decreasing radius, and increasing radius corners (Fig. 7-1).

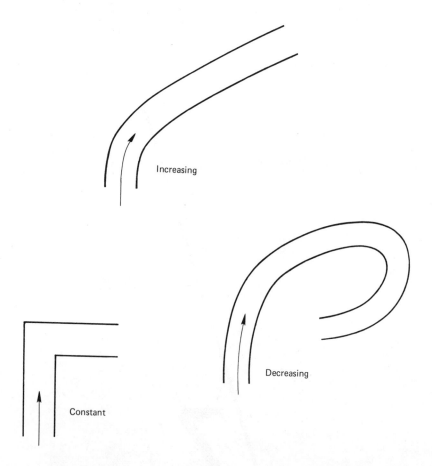

Figure 7-1 Increasing, decreasing, and constant radius corners.

CORNERING

A *constant radius* corner has a radius or "distance from a center line or point to an axis of rotation," as the dictionary puts it, that is constant. A constant radius corner would become a circle if permitted to continue a full 360-degrees around.

A *decreasing radius* corner is a curve in which the turn angle becomes sharper as you drive around it. A good example of a decreasing radius corner can be found on highway underpasses, in which an exit ramp curves around and under the highway.

The third and final type of corner is the *increasing radius* corner. This type of corner requires a sharp turning angle at first, then a gradual straightening. Some freeway access ramps are like this; they begin with a sharp turn required to get off the surface street and onto the freeway, then gradually straighten to allow traffic to speed up and enter the freeway traffic flow smoothly.

Knowing the various corner types is very important, because they all require different types of driving. Of course, knowing how to maneuver around corners is important for all drivers, but for the police officer in hot pursuit of another vehicle, it could spell the difference between life and death.

An overwhelming number of accidents take place at intersections, so control of the car while cornering is vital. As the driver, your job is to drive as efficiently as possible. To do this, you must overcome the tendency of the car to move to the outside of the turn. As an emergency driver, part of your job is to drive through the corner as quickly as possible. The term used in driving school for this move is "fast through the corner." This is not intended to mean how fast you were driving when you entered the corner. Anyone can approach and enter a corner going fast. But to drive safely through a corner as quickly and efficiently as possible requires skill and precision.

In order to do this, drivers need only put as little steering force as possible on the car. Approaching a corner very fast, only to have to slam on the brakes and crawl around the corner, is inefficient, dangerous, and accomplishes nothing.

To drive that corner quickly and efficiently, you'll have to "straighten out the corner," or, in other words, make the path of the car through the corner the biggest radius possible. Remember that in our driving equation—$LA = V^2/R32.2$—R represents the radius of the corner. If the value for R is large, it means the corner

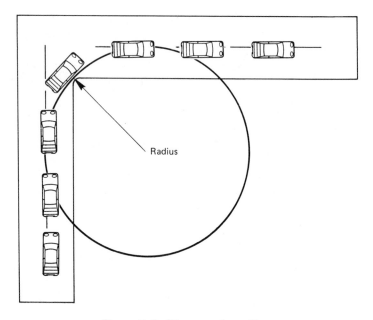

Figure 7-2   Diagram of a radius.

had a larger radius (Fig. 7-2). This type of corner means not a sharp turn, but a gentle, gradual turn, with very little steering force imparted on the vehicle. Because the steering required is slight, the ride through the corner will be a comfortable one. What's more, the larger the corner's radius, the faster it can be driven through.

As you enter a corner, your vehicle should be on the outside of the curve, still in your assigned lane, of course, but to the outside of that lane (refer to Fig. 7-3). Never drive in the oncoming lane, or a lane that rightfully belongs to another car, but do make good use of all the road available to you. Entering the corner, gradually steer your vehicle to the inside of the corner; your inside tire (the tire on the side of the vehicle in the direction you are turning) should ride over an imaginary point on the road known as the "apex," which, depending on the dimensions of the curve itself, will be at some point on the curve's inside path.

As you begin your approach into the curve, aim the car so you will drive over that imaginary apex. Once safely past the apex, the vehicle will return to the outside of the road pretty much by itself.

Once more, the proper procedure for taking a corner at speed is to drive from the outside edge of the road as you enter the corner,

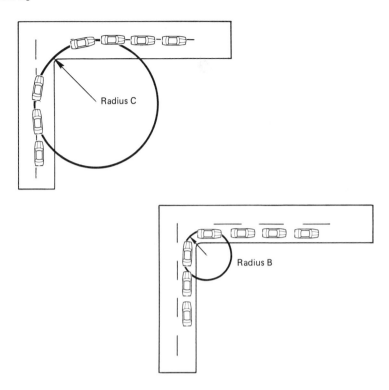

Figure 7-3 Big radius vs. small radius. A car can be driven faster around radius C than it can around radius B.

then move to the inside to intersect the apex, and then back to the outside to exit the corner.

Of course, you must perform this maneuver without driving into the other lane of traffic. In racing this is called "taking a line." The line referred to is the path your vehicle takes as it passes through the corner. Every corner has a line and apex that allows a careful driver to maneuver through it as quickly and efficiently as possible.

For instance, let's look at the average 90-degree street corner, with streets 33 feet wide. We'll drive through it two different ways and get some interesting results. If we take the corner by hugging the inside of the road, we make a 50-foot radius. But if we take the ideal line through this corner, entering on the outside, covering the inside apex, and exiting on the outside, we have driven the largest radius possible: 138 feet. If you wish, you can work out the mathematics of this maneuver with the driving equation given above. What

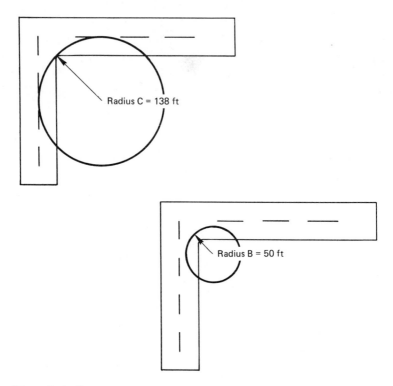

Figure 7-4 Driving a big radius vs. a small radius. Radius C is much bigger than radius B.

is obvious is that it is far easier and quicker to take a corner with a 138-foot radius than a 50-foot radius (see Fig. 7-4).

Where Is the Apex?

Accurately locating the apex of a curve is vital. If you pass over what you thought was the correct apex point too early into the turn, you won't have enough road to complete your turn through the corner, at least not at your present speed. As you exit the corner, you'll either drive off the road or enter another lane.

This "early apex" phenomenon is caused by turning the wheel too soon into the turn. This usually happens when a driver starts the turn as soon as he sees it. Although this is a natural reaction, it's better to wait a little longer and turn the steering wheel a little later. The next time you're cruising your favorite freeway, check out the exit ramps to your right. Notice the frequent tire tracks, all those skid marks? Those marks were made by drivers who entered the exit ramp too fast, turned the wheel too soon, drove through an early apex, and ran out of road by hitting the curb on the outside. Their problem? Picking an early apex.

As you approach a corner, judge the speed at which you feel you can safely enter that corner. Often corner and ramp speeds are posted on highways. Pick a speed that's a little lower than you feel the turn requires. You are not a racing driver trying to blow through the corner while setting a new world's record in the process. You are an emergency driver trying to get through the corner as quickly and safely as you can. *Leave room for error.* You should probably enter the corner at a comparatively slow speed and accelerate in the turn so you come out fast. Never enter a corner as fast as you can and hope that your brakes can slow you down sufficiently for you to survive this experience. If you've already used up your tires' capacity for stopping and then try to use them for control, you're in for a big, nasty, tire-screeching, fender-bending surprise.

WEATHER AND THE ROAD

Along with coping with the variables of road design, drivers must also cope with weather-related road conditions. By far the most frightening and dangerous conditions are ice and snow. Driving in snow can be a white-knuckle experience for even the most experienced drivers. The best advice for driving in snow is *don't.* For police officers and other emergency vehicle drivers, this advice obviously cannot apply. You must drive in the snow; in fact, you'll probably receive some of your most important emergency calls in conditions of bad weather. It's all part of the job.

Although you can't refuse to go out on a call, there are some things you can do to make life a little easier and safer.

First, make sure you can see. Clean all snow from all car windows and mirrors. Don't play "tank commander" and just clear a little slit for you to look through.

Don't drive wearing boots so big they interfere with pedal operation; for instance, wearing a boot so wide that it depresses the brake pedal when the driver thinks the foot is only on the gas. This may sound like a ludicrous recommendation but it's surprising how many highway police do this. Once you've got proper boots on, make certain to keep them clear of clumps of ice or snow that could interfere with pedal use. Snow or ice on the soles of boots can cause them to slide off pedals at critical times.

One of the most frightening experiences in driving is suddenly going from a dry road surface to one that's covered with ice. The experience is analogous to running at full speed and then abruptly discovering you are running on ice. You look like something out of a children's cartoon; your feet are windmilling like mad while your body stays put. Eventually, your feet will shoot out from under you and down you'll come.

All this pretty much holds true for a car on an icy surface. Under dry conditions, your feet are like little car tires. Real car tires grab the surface and propel the car forward. Imagine a car on a dry surface approaching ice. The rear wheels are propelling the vehicle while the front wheels are steering the vehicle (obviously, on front-wheel-drive vehicles, the front wheels are performing both these vital functions). Suddenly, the car encounters ice and none of the tires have any adhesion whatsoever; there is no propulsive or directional control. And, as if this weren't bad enough, it all happens instantly. Any steering or braking you are now contemplating will have to be done as delicately as possible because nearly any control input on ice will result in the vehicle going completely and utterly out of control.

When encountering ice or icy conditions and the need to stop presents itself, or if you find you have to brake and turn, first apply the brakes as lightly as possible. Then release the brakes and steer gently. *Do not try to stop the car by shifting into a lower gear.* When you shift into low gear, the rear wheels can spin and the car will begin to travel sideways. Remember: One of the reasons you are in trouble on ice in the first place is that your wheels are spinning and not creating any traction on a slippery surface. If you put the car in a lower gear, the rear tires spin faster, making the situation worse, not better.

Although driving in rain isn't quite as traumatic as driving in snow, it has terrors of its own. Wet weather of any kind demands a gentle touch with vehicle controls. Rain lowers visibility and creates longer stopping distances. It increases the risks of losing control, especially after radical control movements.

When it rains can be as important as how much it rains. If rain falls after a long dry spell, the road will be far more slippery than if it has been raining regularly for several days. The initial rainfall floats off all the surface oil the road has collected from cars and forms a very slippery suspension that eventually washes away as the rain continues. A merely wet surface can be tricky; an oily wet surface can be deadly.

When driving in rain, here are some simple rules to follow:

- Drive slower than usual. Whether you have to make a high-speed run or not, bear in mind that you do not have the vehicular control you usually do.
- Turn on your headlights if it is raining. This allows other drivers to see you. In some states, the law requires this.
- Turn on your windshield wipers. Make sure they're always in good working order. Don't wait for the next cloudburst to find out your wipers don't work, or that the blades are worn so that they are useless.
- Don't change speed or direction quickly, just as you would never do on ice. This is a sure way to encounter a potentially dangerous skid.

We will examine the question of rain tires in our chapter on tires.

WINTER DRIVING

Wet roads are most slippery when the temperature is near freezing. Solidly frozen ice is the most dangerous. Snow provides better traction than ice if it is not too packed and there's no ice under it.

Encountering different driving surface conditions is especially dangerous in winter. A rapid transition from dry pavement to ice can cause a driver to overreact, or react roughly, with the car's controls, thus throwing the vehicle completely out of control. The first and most obvious solution to driving on ice is to slow down. Very few of us have the presence of mind to do that.

To recover from an ice slide, put the car in neutral, then press gently on the brake pedal. You must be gentle. Do not brake abruptly. Overapplying the brakes will only increase the trouble you're already in. Steer in the direction you want the car to go.

Once you have straightened out, apply a very slight amount of gas. We cannot overemphasize use of a light touch on the controls here. Be careful how much you turn the steering wheel. If you turn it too much and over-correct, the car will begin to fishtail.

Most drivers travel a variety of roads: superhighways, city streets, country roads. Police officers on patrol, however, tend to travel one type of road—over and over and over. State police patrol highways, and in most states they are responsible for the rural areas. As we discussed in the first chapter, state police have the lowest accident rates of all police studied. This is attributable mainly to the types of roads they travel.

Urban patrolling is the most hazardous type of police driving. In bad weather, city police are challenged by the dangers of slippery surfaces in addition to the standard threats of blind intersections, steep hills, bad pavement, potholes, stop-and-go traffic, and wayward pedestrians.

The following is a scenario familiar to those who have had the chance to drive on ice: You cruise around the corner of Main and Elm. It's winter but today is nice and sunny, although cold. You approach the corner at 40 mph, slowing to 20 mph, and turn the wheel approximately 45 degrees. You round the corner successfully, and five seconds later you've forgotten the entire routine maneuver.

The next day, the temperature has dropped 20 degrees and it's snowing heavily. The road is very slippery. You approach the same corner at 40 mph, and attempt to slow to 20 mph. The first sign of trouble comes when you try to slow. Not much happens when you apply the brakes. The car is still traveling forward, a little slower than before, but still traveling. Because of the slippery surface, there is no friction to stop the car.

You turn the steering wheel to the same 45 degrees that worked just fine yesterday. Only this time nothing happens. The car continues traveling in a straight line.

What's the fundamental difference between what worked yesterday and what isn't working today? On yesterday's dry pavement, the tires had sufficient adhesion to propel, control, and stop the vehicle. Today, on a slick surface, the tires lack this adhesion. So what's the answer? Lower the forces involved. How is that done? Remove the source of the force, namely, the vehicle speed and the angle of the turn. Now, we'll be the first to admit that it is rather difficult to drive around a corner without turning the wheel. So that leaves us with but a single answer: *Slow down!* That's it. It's so simple. If the weather has altered the road conditions: slow down. We know this is tough to do in an emergency situation, when you're trying to get to people in trouble. But those people you're trying to reach in such a hurry are depending on your help, and you can't give them that if you demolish your valuable rescue vehicle and yourself on the way to them.

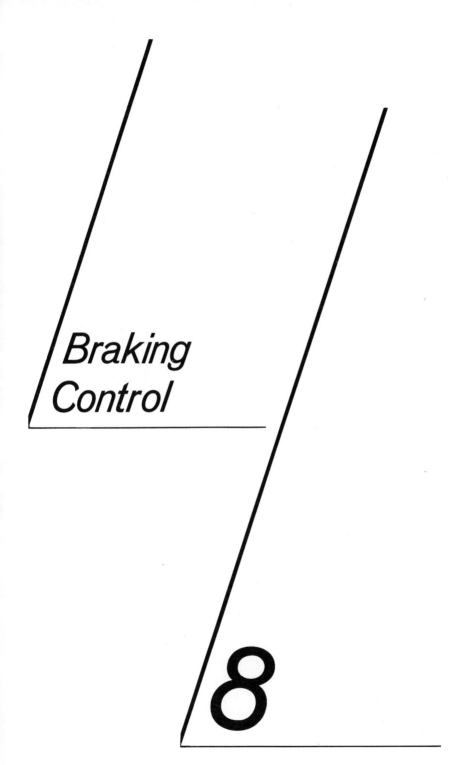

Braking
Control

8

Most police departments consider brakes the single most troublesome component on police vehicles, according to a study conducted by the National Bureau of Standards. Naturally, police organizations that patrol cities, and therefore do a lot of stop-and-go driving, reported greater difficulties with brakes than highway police. Overall, however, brakes emerged as one of the biggest areas of complaint.

Brakes are by far the most important, most sensitive automobile control. Brakes are also the most challenging control to operate. To get a better understanding of brakes, let's look at the dynamics of stopping a vehicle.

HOW CARS STOP

The first thing we need to know is that *brakes don't stop cars*. Brakes stop wheels from rolling. The friction of the tires against the road surface stops the car. If brakes alone stopped cars, then cars would never skid.

The maximum amount of friction between tire and road occurs just before the tire stops rolling. The engineering explanation for this is that rolling friction is greater than sliding friction, or that a tire rolling across pavement has more stopping capability than a tire sliding across pavement.

This is a vital concept, central to the whole dynamic of the moving vehicle. All of us who were taught to drive were told that to stop the car, all we had to do was step on the brakes. What most of us weren't taught was that after a given point, pressing harder on the brake didn't stop the car any quicker. In fact, pressing too hard on the brake could get us into big trouble.

For example, the average male can step on the brake with 140 lb to 185 lb of pressure. The average female can hit the brakes with between 70 lb to 100 lb of pressure. In an emergency situation, if a driver applies 80 lb of pressure to the brake pedal, and in so doing locks the wheels and stops the tires from rolling, that driver has actually created *less* friction between tire and road. If the brakes are applied with 60 lb pressure, enough to slow the car but still allow the wheels to roll, the effect is to create *more* friction between tire and road (see Fig. 8-1). A locked-up, skidding wheel experiences a lower level of friction than does a slowing but still rotating tire. With less friction, more time and distance are required to stop the car. At this point, applying more brake pressure will do nothing but make the situation worse.

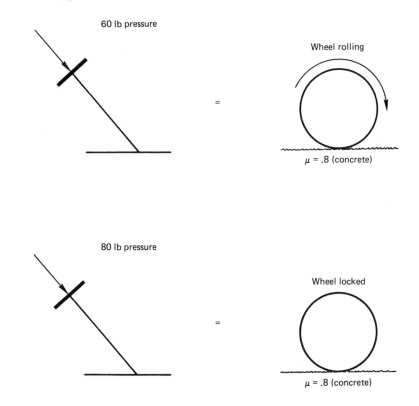

Figure 8-1 Brake pedal pressure and loss of control.

When a vehicle is stopping or slowing down, it has to overcome the momentum that has been built up in the moving car. Just as there is an equation for turning a car, as we saw in Chapter 6, there is also an equation for stopping a car. And, as in Chapter 6, you don't have to memorize the equation, but a quick examination of it can do much to help you understand why stopping a car in certain circumstances is a unique situation. The equation follows:

$$S = V^2/2\ \mu g$$

S, Stopping distance
V, Velocity
μ, Coefficient of friction
g, Acceleration of gravity (32.2)

The Greek letter μ is pronounced "mew." It represents the combination of speed(s) and it can get us into a lot of trouble. From the equation, we can see that the faster we go, the more distance is required for us to stop, and that the lower the value assigned to μ, the more distance required for us to stop.

What's especially disturbing is the fact that as speed is doubled, the distance required to stop safely is quadrupled. For instance, if a car traveling at 20 mph is accelerated to 40 mph, its stopping distance does not increase by a factor of two but by a factor of four.

Look what happens when we change the value for μ in the equation. The value μ changes as the environment changes, and when μ changes, the driving environment can get exciting in a hurry. For instance, if you are driving at 50 mph on a surface with a coefficient of friction (μ) of 0.8 (that of a dry concrete surface), it will require 104 feet to stop the car, not counting driver reaction time.

If the same car is moving at 50 mph when it encounters a surface with a coefficient of friction (μ) of 0.05, the stopping distance increases to 1,688 feet, or a little more than one-third of a mile. Consider the above equation a basic fact of life when it comes to stopping a car. Remember too:

1. The faster the car is traveling, the more distance it needs to stop.
2. Like centrifugal force, speed and stopping distance are not linear. Small changes in speed mean big changes in the distance required to stop safely.
3. If road conditions are slippery, which translates as the coefficient of friction (or value μ of the equation above) decreasing, the required distance for a safe stop will increase dramatically.
4. Those who drive fast on slippery roads will spend a great deal of time in the hospital and/or in court.

There are almost as many ways of braking a car to a stop as there are reasons for stopping. There is the gentle stop at a traffic light and there is the "Oh my God!" sort of life-and-death stop that nearly stops your heart as well as your vehicle. Obviously, the latter type is most likely encountered in emergency situations and is the one we will discuss here.

LOSS OF CONTROL

An analysis of what happens in emergency crash situations shows a very high likelihood of one or more of the vehicles being completely out of control. "Out of control" here means that just before the accident occurred, the vehicle was either spinning or skidding. In many of these situations, excessive braking was identified as the main culprit.

This news that improper braking can easily throw a vehicle out of control comes as a revelation to many drivers, who associate loss of control with harsh or abrupt movements of the steering wheel.

Bear in mind just what loss of control really is. No control means that the driver is not and cannot predict the path the car will follow. The car moves as if it had a mind of its own, spinning, skidding, and sliding. Actually, the car is responding to the laws of physics and of motion, but those responses can look pretty random to the innocent bystander.

Loss of control frequently occurs in emergency situations. We will assume, for purpose of discussion, that the driver's reaction to this control loss will be hard, excessive braking. Hard braking in a contemporary automobile means the application of 50 to 100 lb of pressure. How hard should the brakes be applied in an emergency? It's not easy to provide an answer that's correct for all situations because of the many variables involved. The same amount of brake pressure that brings you to a safe and comfortable stop on a dry pavement can throw you completely out of control on an icy road surface. So much depends on the coefficient of friction, and on drivers developing their own base of experience. The techniques used to stop a car as quickly and safely as possible cannot be learned simply by reading a book. That's why we have emergency driving schools.

The method preferred by professional instructors is known as "controlled braking." This technique calls for pressure to be applied on the brake pedal almost up to the point of lock-up. At the same time, drivers must be aware that the more brake pressure applied, the less steering leeway they will have.

Let's take a step-by-step look at the braking process:

1. The steering wheel is pointing the car's front wheels straight ahead.
2. The driver applies 50 lb of pedal pressure.
3. The front wheels reach their point of optimal road friction, the point just before they lock up and cease rolling.
4. Unfortunately, by this time there isn't enough room between the car and the obstacle that was the reason for applying the

brakes in the first place. The driver sees that a collision is almost unavoidable.

5. In a further effort to avoid the collision, the driver turns the wheel.

6. Although the steering wheel is movable, a slight movement of that wheel will cause the front wheels to lock up, rendering steering completely ineffective.

Controlled braking works well in theory, but theories have a way of being forgotten in the real world. When driving, always bear in mind that a panic-inducing, serious emergency situation can occur anytime. When that happens, drivers find themselves doing a not-so-hot job of controlled braking. In fact, they really mess up, locking the front wheels while turning the steering wheel and making the front end swerve.

Think of all this as a religious experience. At this point, your only salvation is to get that foot off the brakes. Once you have locked up your front wheels and subsequently decided that getting out of the path of the oncoming obstacle is your single goal in life, you must take your foot off the brakes in order to get back the steering control you need to make that goal a reality.

BRAKE FADE

While not common in passenger cars, *brake fade* can often happen on police vehicles. Brake fade occurs when brakes are overused and over-heated. Hot brakes quickly lose their effectiveness and fail to stop the car in time. Brake fade comes and goes. Brakes take time to over-heat and will often provide warning that they are about to fade. Effectiveness decreases slowly. If you were in a hot pursuit and noticed your brakes didn't take hold quite as well on the last corner as they did on the one before, you may have detected brake fade. No matter the circumstances, brake fade makes it advisable to slow down or even discontinue the pursuit. Brake fade goes away as the brakes cool. This often confuses drivers who experience brake fade. Sometimes they lose their brakes because of brake fade and run their cars off the road and into the brush. Shaken but unscathed, they later return to their vehicles with a repair crew, only to find their brakes in mysteriously good working order. This is brake fade.

EMERGENCY BRAKING

Probably the most frightening thing that can happen to a driver is to lose braking control completely. Imagine it: You push down on the pedal and nothing, absolutely nothing, happens. The car just keeps on going. This situation calls for a quick decision, especially if you are in busy traffic, such as a crowded street, or surrounded by plenty of large objects with which you could collide.

Your best option is to stay with your vehicle, steering to avoid obstacles, using low gear to slow the vehicle, and seeking a path of escape. Using the parking brake is an option, but the parking brake only stops the rear wheels. If you do decide to use the parking brake, apply it slowly, keeping the front wheels pointed straight ahead. Any movement of the wheel while applying the parking brake will spin the car around 180 degrees.

If all this braking technique sounds like something you should practice, it is. The questions are: where and when? The time to experiment with your car's braking characteristics is not while in an emergency situation. If you happen to live in an area that gets ice and snow in the winter, find a big, empty parking lot, such as those at shopping malls or large supermarkets, and practice. See how hard you can press on the brake pedal without locking up the wheels. Watch out for light stanchions and parked cars (we said find an *empty* lot), but otherwise take it easy and carefully play with your car. Discover its limitations and abilities.

A great deal of the success of the various emergency braking maneuvers depend on the driver's alertness and powers of observation. When driving, you should be looking ahead; indeed, you should mentally *be* ahead of your car by at least six seconds. At 30 mph, a six-second eye lead means your eyes should be focused at least 285 feet in front of the car.

Sadly, when driving in traffic, most untrained drivers are focused so closely that they only react to the brake lights of the car in front of them. When the driver in front hits the brakes, so do they. Sometimes they're too late. If you ask these brake-light followers why they persist in this strange habit, they'll invariably tell you, "I can't see around the car in front of me, so I have to react to that car's brake lights." These people are evidently not bright enough to realize that the reason they cannot see around the car in front of them is because they are following the car too closely. If the vehicle they are following is a large one, such as a tractor-trailer, it only makes matters worse.

As a police officer, you must maintain a safe distance between your vehicle and the vehicle in front of you. It reflects badly on both you and your department if you rear-end a vehicle.

The issue of proper following distance becomes worse when vehicles approach an intersection equipped with traffic lights. Most motorists think the yellow "caution" signal of a traffic light means, "Hurry up! Floor it before the light turns red." But when they look in their rear-view mirror and see a police cruiser, it's another story. When those drivers see the police behind them, they stand on their brakes and try to stop before entering the intersection. They're afraid that if they get caught crossing the intersection when the light turns red, they'll get a ticket for running a red light. Here's the scenario:

A motorist (in car A) is driving at 30 mph and a police cruiser (car B) is following at the same speed, some 30 feet behind (see Fig.

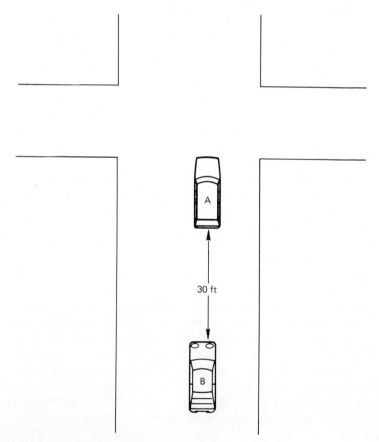

Figure 8-2 Stopping vs. reaction time.

8-2). Both cars approach an intersection and the light changes to yellow. The motorist hits the brakes. The officer in the cruiser is not paying as much attention as needed and allows a full second to pass before starting to react to the situation. Once the motorist applies the brakes, it will require about 55 feet to stop that 30-mph car. Thus, a stopped car is 85 feet in front of the cruiser, and if the cruiser is doing 30 mph, it is moving at 44 ft/sec. Assuming a normal reaction time of 0.75 seconds, and adding the fact that the officer's attention was diverted for one second, means the officer will not get a foot to the brake pedal before having traveled 77 feet. A collision is inevitable.

If the front of the motorist's stopped car is 85 feet from the cruiser's starting point, and that car is 15 feet long, then its rear end is just 70 feet away from the cruiser's front end. Because it's going to take 77 feet before the officer gets a foot to the brake, everyone involved is in for a whole lot of trouble.

If the same example is examined once more and that one second of diverted attention eliminated, an accident is still the outcome. The officer applies the brakes the instant the motorist's brake lights are observed. The rear end of that car is still 70 feet from the cruiser's front end. How long does it take to stop at 30 mph?

The answer is it takes 88 feet to come to a complete halt. That isn't enough, and an accident is the result. The problem? The cruiser was following too closely.

FOLLOWING TOO CLOSELY

All the fancy braking techniques in the world won't help if you follow other vehicles too closely. Use the "two-second rule." Always leave two seconds between you and the car ahead of you. Pick a fixed object on the road, and when the car ahead of you has passed it, count out two seconds. When the two seconds are up, you should pass that object. If you pass it before the two seconds, you're driving too closely.

Some folks argue that it's important to drive close to the car in front of you because if you don't, someone will get in between the two of you and cut off the second vehicle. This is ridiculous for a number of reasons, but let's look at why it's ridiculous from a law-enforcement point of view. First of all, you're on patrol, not in a race. Unless you're on an emergency call, in which case you'd have your lights, flashers, and siren on, you've got no reason to be in a hurry. Secondly, not too many people are in a hurry to cut off a police cruiser in traffic, just for the sake of getting ahead of it.

So, our objective when it comes to following traffic is simple: Keep a safe distance between you and the vehicle ahead.

OTHER HAZARDS

Vehicles aren't your only problem while on urban patrol. Pedestrians are potential challenges to your driving skills as well. The most practical way you have of communicating with both pedestrians and drivers is your horn.

In an urban setting, people are prone to backing out of parking spaces without looking to see what's there. If they are heading toward you, a gentle toot on your horn will inform them that you are there and would greatly appreciate it if they would not back into you.

In a similar vein, if you are stopped at an intersection waiting to make a left turn, keep your front wheels pointed straight until it's time to make that turn. Why? Simple. If your wheels are turned left, and you are hit from the rear, your car will be pushed to the left because of the direction the front wheels are pointed. This move would put you directly in the path of oncoming traffic, and you would face a possible collision even more serious than the first.

The point being made here is easy to understand and very fundamental to safe driving: *Leave yourself an out. Have an escape route for every move you make.*

To do this, you have to be aware of what's going on around you all the time. Your best tools for doing this are your mirrors, both rear and side view. Too many of us only use our rearview mirrors when we want to pull out into traffic. Use all your mirrors in order to get the big picture; have accurate information about what's happening on your right, left, and rear. In an emergency situation, such as a collision right in front of you, you need all the information you can get about what's happening around you and you need it fast. Mirrors are your best way of getting this information.

Your car should be fitted with right-side mirrors adjustable from the driver's seat. You should not have to reach across the vehicle to adjust the right-side mirror.

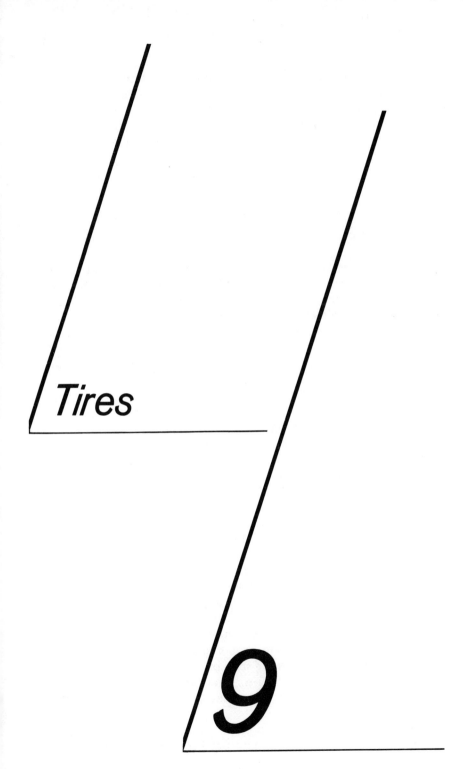

Tires

9

By now it should be apparent that, along with brakes, the tires are among a vehicle's most important components. The quality of control you maintain over your vehicle is only as good as the tires that are on your vehicle. A vehicle with outstanding handling qualities can have those qualities negated by poor or inferior tires.

Tires must be treated with care. Underinflation of tires and misalignment of the car's suspension system are the most common forms of tire mistreatment.

TIRE INFLATION

Figure 9-1 shows how tires look with various amounts of inflation. Underinflation prematurely wears tires. The rule of thumb is that a single pound of underinflation takes 600 miles off a tire's life. Most tires only last 70 percent of their design life, thanks to underinflation.

If the tires on your car aren't properly inflated, you're not only wasting tires but you're also wasting hundreds of miles' worth of gasoline. This is because a properly inflated tire offers less rolling resistance than one that's underinflated; thus, it requires more energy to roll an underinflated tire than one with the proper amount of air in it. And remember, in an automobile, energy is gasoline. On the average, cars lose mileage at the rate of about a half mile per gallon if the tires fall 6 lb below a recommended inflation of 32 lb per square inch (psi).

Underinflated tires not only wear out more quickly and are a drain on gasoline mileage but they also exhibit less overall durability and can be more easily damaged.

As a general rule, inflate tires to the pressure recommended by the tire manufacturer, adding four extra pounds of air per tire if sustained freeway driving is anticipated.

Tire types make a difference. Radial tires have two-thirds the rolling resistance of a cross or bias-ply tire. Beyond 40,000 miles, a properly inflated radial tire pays for itself.

As a tire ages, it's easy to tell if it's been underinflated for much of its life. If the tire is worn on the outside edges, it's been underinflated. Keeping tires at the proper pressure is easy. Tire pressure gauges are inexpensive and fit in a pocket. Compressed air is available at almost every gas station. The hardest part to keeping tires properly inflated is simply taking the few moments required to do the job.

Low tire pressure gives a car a "softer" ride, because the tires act much like a spring. With low pressure, the tire is a soft spring;

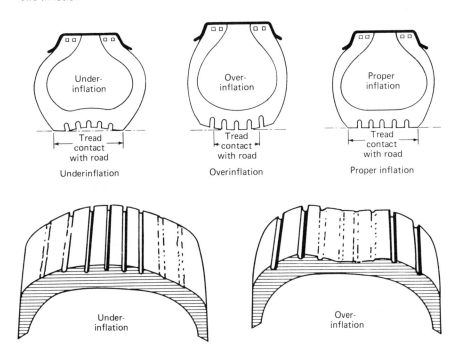

Figure 9-1 Tire pressure inflation.

with high pressure, it is like a hard spring, producing a hard ride. For proper vehicle handling in police driving, you want properly inflated tires, no matter how hard they may feel. This is because the amount of air in a tire determines the amount of load that tire can safely accept. If your tires are type 185-15, it means that if your tire has 20 psi worth of air inside it, it will accept a maximum of 1,000 lb of force. If the pressure in that same tire is increased to 32 psi, it will take 1,420 lb. Expressed simply, an underinflated tire cannot accept the sort of load that emergency driving puts on it. It is far easier to lose control of the vehicle on underinflated tires.

In examining a typical tire, we encounter some interesting facts:

1. Tire pressure affects the tire's ability to corner. The sharper the turn required by a corner, the more effect tire pressure has. This is because a sharp turn puts more stress on a tire than a gentle turn, and an underinflated tire accepts less stress before losing its grip on the pavement and going out of control.

2. A tire rated for inflation to 32 psi but only carrying 24 psi loses 10 percent of its handling capability on sharp turns. Remember that a car is a weight-bearing machine. Every time you move the

controls, you are shifting weight throughout the vehicle. These shifts are all eventually felt at the tires. The tires' ability to bear that weight is dependent on tire pressures.

When tires get sick, they show their drivers a number of symptoms in plenty of time for the tires to be "cured." By learning to read the early warning signs, you can prevent the problems that not only shorten tire life by thousands of miles but also make those tires unsafe to drive on.

As we have said, when a tire is underinflated, most of its road contact is on the outer tread ribs, which causes the outside edge of the tire to wear faster than the middle. With overinflation, the opposite wear pattern appears. The center tread area bulges out slightly, causing it to wear faster than the outer ribs.

If you are driving a car equipped with a set of the new P-metric tires, which will eventually replace the alphanumeric size tires, you should know that the P-metric tire pressures can be exceeded by 2 or 3 psi over the recommended pressures listed in the owner's manual or on the placard usually found in the glove compartment. Not only can you exceed those pressures by a small amount but P-metric tires are inflated to a higher pressure overall. Inflation pressures are determined by the automaker and are based on the car's weight and the anticipated load it will carry. However, it is difficult for automakers to figure out exactly how much weight will be transferred to the front of the car during heavy braking. So a perfect tire pressure for all conditions is nearly impossible to come up with.

State police and other law-enforcement officers who spend a lot of time in prolonged freeway or expressway driving should increase tire pressure 4 lb over the car manufacturer's recommended pressure—as long as that pressure doesn't exceed their maximum psi figure printed on the tire sidewall.

It's vitally important to keep track of the amount of air in your tires. Ideally, you should check it before every patrol. As we've seen, the amount of air in the tires affects the vehicle's ability to maneuver safely for it controls the tires' ability to accept the various loads encountered in high-speed pursuit maneuvers. If you were suddenly called upon to enter into a chase and were driving a vehicle with badly underinflated tires, the result could be an accident, injuries, or worse.

Some points to remember about tire pressure:

1. Tire pressures affect fuel consumption. Properly inflated tires are part of the fuel economy equation. If a tire intended to be

inflated to 32 psi is inflated to 24 psi, the result is a 20 percent boost in fuel consumption.

2. If you routinely drive at a sustained speed of 60 mph, you can increase tire pressure by:
   - 4 psi in a radial tire
   - 5.5 psi in a bias-belted tire
   - 7 psi in a bias tire

TIRE LONGEVITY

As a car is driven, the rear wheels press down on the pavement. At 30 mph, the rear tires exert a 5-horsepower (hp) push against the pavement. At 50 mph, some 16 hp are exerted, and by 70 mph, this number has risen to 38 hp.

What this means is that the faster you drive, the faster you'll wear out your tires. Temperature also has an extreme effect on tires. Low temperatures, or changes in temperature, wear out tires faster. Tests have shown that a change from a winter temperature such as 41 degrees Fahrenheit to a hot summer temperature of 95 degrees Fahrenheit increases tire wear 400 percent, all other conditions being equal.

Tire longevity depends on what type of material the tire is belted with. In radial tire designs, nylon-belted tires last only half as long as their steel-belted counterparts.

There's been a great deal of controversy about the use of steel-belted tires for police work. The simple fact is that steel-belted tires are not unsafe, but that they are unsafe if used improperly. Questions about steel-belted tires began with the failure of some tires during high-speed pursuits. Two of these incidents resulted in the deaths of police officers. Investigations showed that these tires were not speed-rated and simply could not survive sustained high-speed driving. If your department buys tires that are speed-rated, radials should serve you well.

WORN TIRES

Worn tires are trouble. If you're driving on worn tires, you're driving without the tread depth that controls stopping, acceleration, and cornering. When driving on worn tires, you've thrown away some of the control you should have over your vehicle.

Worn tires are prone to hydroplaning, are much more susceptible to puncture, and could otherwise be hazardous to your safety.
Studies by several auto safety organizations, among them the National Bureau of Standards, reveal that cars riding on tires with less
than one-sixteenth of an inch of tread are up to 44 times more likely
to experience a blowout.

More than just unsafe, worn tires are often illegal. The Tire Industry Safety Council reports that 30 states now have laws on the
books requiring that automobile tires have at least one-sixteenth of
an inch of tread; anything less and the driver is issued a summons.

Tires manufactured for police use are different from everyday
tires. In a recent conversation with engineers at Goodyear Tire &
Rubber Co., the following questions were asked about police tires.
Here are the questions, along with the engineers' answers:

1. *How are police tires different from civilian passenger car tires?*
   There is a significant difference. High-performance passenger car
   tires are closely related to police tires in that they both enjoy
   superior handling and high-speed characteristics. A certified
   police tire carries a notarized certification letter from the manufacturer for each tire size and type, certifying the tire's high-
   speed capability. This certified rating is usually up to 130 mph
   or what's known as an "H" speed rating.

2. *Are there any significant differences in overall wear between
   passenger tires and police tires?* Tires in police service exhibit
   faster wear overall, when examined alongside similar tires in service on average passenger cars. The obvious reason is that police
   tires are just plain driven harder; with more fast cornering, rapid
   starts and stops, and much faster driving speeds. City police
   generally wear out tires faster than highway patrols because of
   these obvious environmental driving condition differences.

3. *What's the best belting material for police tires?* While there are
   several good belting materials, the trend is toward steel belts in
   the latest generation of police tires because of steel's inherently
   better handling qualities.

4. *What are your thoughts on the steel-belted police tire controversy?* In 1975, two patrolmen were killed in unrelated high-
   speed chases when their tires failed. In both cases, the tires on
   their vehicles were standard passenger car tires not certified for
   police use. Because all certified police tires at that time were
   fabric-belted, the blame fell on the belt material rather than on
   the lack of certification. Any tire, regardless of belt material,

not certified for high-speed application, is subject to failure when used beyond the limits for which it was designed. It is of utmost importance that all police agencies use only tires certified for police and high-speed use.

5. *Is there any difference between the kind of tire you'd recommend for highway patrol vs. city police work?* No. Police tires exhibit significantly better handling and traction characteristics than most passenger tires and should be important to city police for that reason alone.

6. *What advice would you offer to police departments interested in prolonging the life of their tires?* Maintain the maximum allowable air pressure and check it frequently. Also, tires should be rotated on a frequent basis when the vehicles are in for routine maintenance.

TIRES AND INCLEMENT WEATHER

The purpose of tires is to create the road friction needed to do the things that can be done with cars; such as go, stop, and turn. However, nasty things like changes in the weather can prevent tires from doing these things. When the ground is covered with water, a good tire design swallows that water into the tread pattern and pushes it out to the sides of the tires. Some tires do this better than others, and these are called *all-weather tires.* Snow tires are completely different and require a different sort of design. All tire designs are compromises of some sort, surrendering one advantage in order to gain another. All-weather tires won't be as good as snow tires on some types of snow, and they won't be better than performance tires in high-performance use. They may not even last as long as long-life passenger tires, but all-weather tires are still better than all the others in matching the broad variety of driving conditions encountered in the U.S.

Regular passenger car tires should not be used on patrol cars that may be involved in pursuits. Passenger car tires simply are not designed to be driven at high speeds. In a survey conducted by the International Association of Chiefs of Police, 38.9 percent of the departments use high-speed pursuit tires. A pursuit tire is one capable of sustained speeds of 125 mph. Many department chiefs have a problem with the term "pursuit tire" because they think the only time such a tire will be useful is in a high-speed pursuit. This is not so. The pursuit tire is a better-built tire that can render superior service at many different speeds and in many different conditions.

Should you use snow tires on your cruiser? Yes. In some parts of the U.S. it's practically mandatory to have snow tires installed on your car. However, snow tire problems can arise when the tires are left on the vehicle too long after the snow season has passed. Driving on snow tires for prolonged periods on dry pavement results in greatly diminished gas mileage. What's more, the rubber formulated for use on snow tires becomes soft and deteriorates during warm weather.

But the most important drawback to snow tires comes in the area of driving performance; they simply do not have the cornering performance of conventional tires. A car equipped with snow tires in the rear and conventional tires up front is much more likely to go out of control in a high-performance situation. Even worse, snow tires are not as good at stopping the car as conventional tires.

Let's get an idea of some tire basics. There are three things that determine how a tire works:

1. The chemical compound of the rubber.
2. The tire's construction: whether it is bias, bias-belted, or radial ply.
3. The tread design, whether snow, all-weather, or conventional-type passenger tires.

The more rubber in contact with the road, the more traction we have—up to a point. That is why many police cruisers have tires wider than more conventional passenger cars. If we could guarantee that no rain or snow would ever fall, and that roads would never get slippery, then we could use racing slicks (tires with no tread whatsoever) on police cruisers. Racing tire rubbers include a compound that produces a maximum amount of friction with the road. But if it rains, these tires are useless.

DRIVER ABUSE

Picture it: Your car is stuck in mud or in snow, or on a patch of ice. If your first reaction is to shove the "pedal to the metal" and spin the tire free, you're only asking for more trouble, some of it quite serious.

If a driver abuses a tire by spinning it at extremely high speeds, the tire can overheat and fail. The worst-case scenario for this situation is a catastrophic tire failure, resulting in tire detonation and the possibility of a dangerous shower of hot rubber. Heat is a tire's worst enemy. A spinning tire creates friction that produces tremendous amounts of heat. This heat, combined with the forces produced by spinning, could cause the tire to fail.

In such a situation, most drivers don't realize just how fast their tires are spinning. A spinning tire's speed is often twice that displayed on the speedometer. Here's why: If one tire is spinning and the other is in a situation that doesn't allow it to spin, the spinning tire will receive the engine's total power output because the car's differential will transfer the engine's power to the point of least resistance. So if the speedometer reads 60 mph, the tire is really spinning at 120 mph.

As if this weren't bad enough, spinning the tires doesn't get the car free. Spinning the tires makes the road surface slicker by melting snow, which then refreezes as ice and also creates ruts that can further complicate the process of freeing the car.

Spinning wheels don't free cars. Peak traction is generated at very low speeds. Once a tire is spinning 15 percent faster than the car is moving, maximum traction has been lost. Increased tire speed is not going to create traction.

To free a trapped car, briefly rock the vehicle, tow it, or apply a traction aid such as sand or ashes or kitty litter to the surface under the tire.

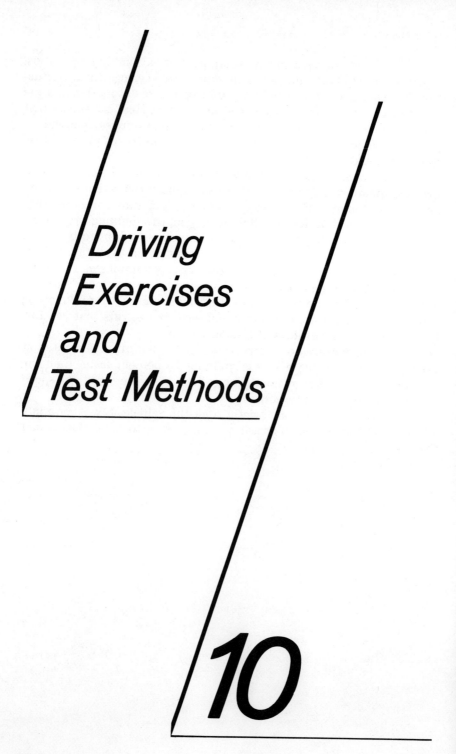

Driving Exercises and Test Methods

10

Does driver training really work? A recent report from the Insurance Institute claimed that defensive driving-training programs have done little, if anything, to prevent driving accidents. What many educators describe as a "defensive driving course" is in reality an eight-hour classroom course using audiovisual materials to explain space cushions, stopping distances, and various accident-avoidance procedures. More often than not, no time is spent in a real car on an actual road. For police officers, such a course is better than nothing, but not much better, as the Insurance Institute points out.

DRIVER-TRAINING PROGRAMS

There is no way to teach drivers how to control cars in an emergency other than to actually get in a car and drive through an emergency situation. The exclusively classroom approach is like trying to teach someone to be a football star by showing slides of O.J. Simpson in action. Most police departments offer a classroom-only defensive-driving course, the kind in which the instructor drones on and on in a lecture accompanied by slides of defensive-driving techniques. This sort of classroom is usually a very quiet place, the only sounds coming from the instructor, the fan on the slide projector, and the gentle snoring of the students.

Some police departments teach an emergency-operator's course with hands-on training and a curriculum that treats the problems of police driving in depth. When the results from the two different classroom approaches are compared, the results are impressive. Officers who have taken the emergency driver program with hands-on training had significantly fewer accidents than those officers who had not taken the course.

So does driver training work? The answer is an unqualified yes, as long as it's the proper training. Just what do police officers need to learn? They need to learn and develop skills in automobile control, along with a basic understanding of vehicle dynamics, the legal ramifications of operating an emergency vehicle, and, above all, how to develop and maintain the proper attitude.

The first and best place to start is with the instructors. Instructors must be of the highest quality. They must understand and be able to explain every phase of the program. They must be able to communicate difficult and complex concepts. They must be able to explain to the students why they are performing a certain exercise and how that exercise relates to police driving.

Driver training will not prevent all police-driving accidents. Many police accidents are minor, low-speed, fender-bender mishaps caused not by a lack of skill or instruction but by plain old brain fade. A skilled driver who drives without paying the fullest attention is driving without the benefit of the skills he or she worked so hard to assimilate. Little can be done about these types of minor, troublesome accidents except to change the driver's attitudes and develop their skills. And that can best be done in a well-conceived, professionally run driver-training program.

Most behind-the-wheel driver-training programs are similar. Most are designed to teach both emergency handling techniques and routine day-to-day driving habits.

For this reason, driver training must create "emergency" situations in a controlled environment. As students drive through these simulated emergencies, they develop their decision-making abilities. They're able to make better decisions far faster than they ever could before. Development of the decision-making process is extremely important. In an emergency, most of us revert to reflexes and training, which is another word for experience. One of the reasons astronauts spend so much time "flying" spacecraft simulators is that by experiencing every conceivable sort of horrendous emergency in the simulator they will have developed decision-making capabilities to draw on if the real emergency ever does happen. They'll spend less time being surprised by the emergency and more time dealing with it, rationally and calmly. Because the astronauts have been in every possible emergency situation before, made even more impressive by a very sophisticated and realistic training simulator, they almost instinctively know what to do. And that's what training is all about.

Some of the actions we take in a real emergency driving situation are reactions we've learned during training. These reactions are:

- Application of the brakes.
- Turning the steering wheel.
- Using both brakes and the steering wheel.

DRIVING EXERCISES

Changes in speed and the ways these changes can affect drivers' abilities to use brakes and/or steering must be addressed in any training program. Training at this point consists of driving through a series of controlled exercises.

Figure 10-1   Vehicle driving through slalom.

One of these exercises is called the *slalom* (Fig. 10-1). In the training area, a number of orange safety cones are set up in a straight line and separated by equal distances. The drivers enter the course and weave back and forth between the cones at various speeds. The exercise is one of the best ways to teach drivers how speed affects maneuverability. In fact, the serpentine can be used to teach many of the basic driving techniques (Fig. 10-2).

The objectives of the serpentine include the following:

1. *Proper seating and steering wheel hand positions.*
2. *Weight transfer.* This is a good time to explain how centrifugal force works. The vehicle will exhibit a great deal of body lean as it is driven through the exercise course (Fig. 10-3).
3. *Space/time concepts.* If the driver enters the serpentine at 40 mph and the cones are separated by 60 feet, the driver has about one full second to react between cones. If there are more than four cones, driving through them at 40 mph will prove very difficult. With four cones separated by 60 feet, it should take about three seconds to drive through the serpentine at 40 mph.
4. *Differences in handling in relation to speed.* As speed increases, students notice a big difference in how the car reacts to their

Slalom

1. Develop the proper seating position.
2. Increase the ability to perceive spatial
   relationships with fixed object.
3. Refine timing by processing steering inputs.
4. Develop hand and eye coordination.
5. Learn the concept of feet per second.
6. Introduce the basics of vehicle dynamics.
7. Learn steering skills that will be needed in
   more complicated exercises.

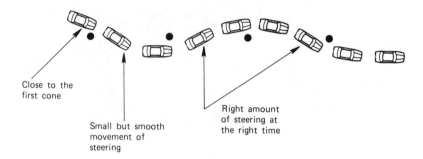

Close to the
first cone

Small but smooth
movement of
steering

Right amount
of steering at
the right time

Figure 10-2   Explanation and diagram of slalom course.

Figure 10-3   Weight transfer on vehicle in slalom.

control inputs. This helps acquaint them with the fundamentals of vehicle dynamics. At some point, they'll see how a small change in speed can result in a very big change in handling.

5. *Awareness of the importance of the front tires.* In high-speed runs through the slalom the tires may be stressed to the point where they're very nearly riding on their rims. During the turns (and in the slalom there's virtually nothing other than turns) one front tire is pushed down so forcefully that it becomes ineffective as a controlling device, while the other tire is being lifted nearly off the ground by the sharp turn, rendering it ineffective as well. Caused by the weight transfer inherent in a severely-maneuvered vehicle, this creates a tremendous amount of understeer (see Chapter 6). By the time the final cone flashes past, the driver will have turned the steering wheel a great deal but the car will want to go straight.

6. *An intuitive feel for the speed and large steering wheel movements that can create powerful forces acting on the car.* The forces cause shifts in the car's weight distribution, which can cause drivers to lose control.

7. *The importance of timing.* At 35 mph, the vehicle moves 51.5 ft/sec. If a driver takes three-tenths of a second longer than usual to move the steering wheel, that hesitation consumes 15.4 feet. If the slalom is set up so that the cones are 60 feet apart, that hesitation has cost the driver 25 percent of the available distance. If a driver hesitates in reacting at the wheel, it can cost a great deal of distance.

CONTROLLED BRAKING

It is absolutely imperative that all police officers learn how to stop a car quickly and under full control. Braking exercises (Fig. 10-4) must teach the following:

1. How to control a car under heavy braking.
2. Why brake-locked wheels are extremely dangerous.
3. How to use threshold braking. This is accomplished by teaching officers how to press the brake pedal up to the point where the wheels are almost stopped. This produces maximum traction.
4. How to unlock brake-locked front wheels and regain lost control. This isone of the most important skills to be learned.

Braking and Turning

1. Learn to control the vehicle under heavy braking.
2. Experience the hazards of wheel lockup.
3. Train the student to regain control of a vehicle once the front wheels are locked.
4. Experience and control the rapid change in handling characteristics caused by front wheel lockup.

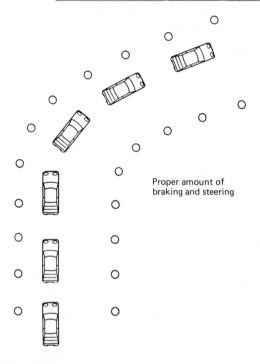

Proper amount of braking and steering

Figure 10-4   Explanation and diagram of controlled braking exercise.

5. The fact that stopping distance increases geometrically while automobile speed increases arithmetically. In braking exercises, use of a stop watch and radar gun can facilitate the establishment of an exercise baseline.

6. Emphasize the amount of time it takes to reach the brake pedal in an emergency and translate that time into meaningful distance figures applicable to the speeds driven by the students in their exercises. This way they learn the impact of reaction time in a realistic fashion.

7. Demonstrate how much weight is transferred from the rear of the car forward under heavy braking (Fig. 10-5).

Figure 10-5   Weight transfer of car under braking.

EVASIVE MANEUVERS

Police officers need to recognize the dangers posed by objects suddenly discovered to be in the path of the cruiser they are driving, to
realize that time is required to identify the danger, to make a decision to alter the car's trajectory, and to execute an evasive maneuver.
Officers must know they do not have to rely solely on their brake
pedal to get them out of trouble, that the steering wheel is also a
useful trouble-evading device (Fig. 10-6).

In many cases, it's far easier to maneuver around an object than
to stop before hitting it. Simple lane change exercises are useful for
teaching this skill. In lane changes, drivers learn about:

1. The time and distance required to make decisions.
2. How the amount of time available for decision making and maneuvering varies with speed.
3. The handling effects of weight shifts in the vehicle during evasive maneuvers.

Backing Up Exercises

The number of police vehicle accidents that occur while the car
is in reverse gear is staggering. Driver-training programs must include
backing-up exercises (Fig. 10-7) that do the following:

Evasive Maneuver

1. Evaluate your reaction time.
2. Understand the concept of feet/per second.
3. Learn not to rely on brakes to avoid an emergency.
4. Understand the relationship between fixed objects and the time required to make a decision.
5. Understand the importance of smoothness and concentration.
6. Learn to combine the proper amount of braking and steering to avoid obstacles.
7. Become aware of the relationship between time and distance.

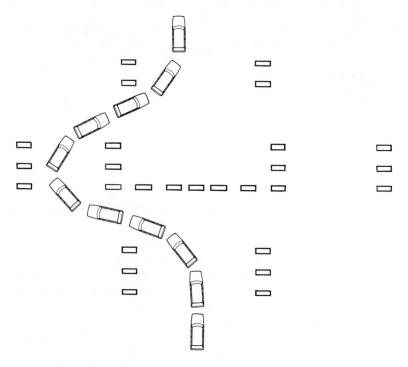

Figure 10-6   Diagram and explanation of evasive maneuver.

1. Train the student to maintain constant rearward vision.

2. Discuss caster angle and why it makes backing up so difficult.

3. Let the driver know how easy it is to lose control.

4. Educate drivers to the fact that they do not have to make large movements with the steering wheel to trigger radical movements in their vehicles.

Backing Up Slalom

> 1. Learn to control the vehicle while
>   traveling backwards.
> 2. Understand the vehicle dynamics involved
>   with backing up.
> 3. Learn to maintain constant vision to
>   the rear.

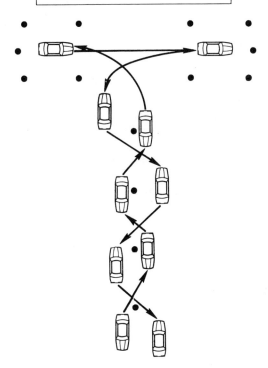

Figure 10-7   Diagram and explanation of backing-up exercise.

DRIVING RANGES

Range Instructors

The range instructors, those personnel actually on duty on the driving range while students are doing their work, must understand all phases of the driving-instruction program, not just the portion they teach. They must be able to communicate difficult concepts in the sometimes-stressful driving-range environment. Range instructors must be able to analyze trainee deficiencies, present these problems to trainees in a nonthreatening manner, and then develop and encourage the trainees in a remedial skill-development program. Not all students are created equal; some need more time to develop than others.

Range instructors must be patient and understand that range instruction is physically tiring, repetitious, and, for some, occasionally a little frightening. As the instructors become more and more involved in the program, they should be encouraged to offer suggestions and input on any program changes or additions they might consider helpful.

Range instructors should not be self-taught but instead be initially trained by other instructors. Self-taught instructors inevitably develop misconceptions and inefficient teaching techniques. It is far better if new range instructors receive guidance and training from experienced instructors before they go on to teach the program themselves.

The Federal Law Enforcement Center in Glynco, Ga., runs the best police instructors' program available. If possible, your range instructors should attend this program.

Range Characteristics

The location you select for your actual driving exercises is very important. Potential range sites include:

1. Commercial or public parking lots, approximately 600 ft X 600 ft. An area this size will allow several exercises to be set up at the same time. Areas smaller than the dimensions listed above are usable as training ranges but the training speeds will have to be lower.
2. Infield areas of raceway ovals or alongside drag strips make ideal locations. Just be careful of the retaining walls and fences that abound in such sites. You don't want your students to start bouncing their cars off of them.
3. Unused airport runways. The New York City Police Department conducts a driving school on the spacious and abandoned runways of long-defunct Floyd Bennett Field.

Safety should be the most important criterion in site selection. Examine your proposed range location with the view that anything that can go wrong will go wrong. Be prepared for any eventuality.

Obviously, the location should be free of obstructions, such as lightpoles, power stanchions, raised curbs, and parking lot dividers. Bear in mind Newton's first law of motion: a body in motion tends

to stay in motion. You don't want the path of that motion to intersect a lightpole or a brick wall. Design exercises so that if something
goes wrong, there's nothing for the driver to hit.

Be mindful of the surrounding neighborhood. Block the range
off so there's no way for a member of the general public to drive
onto the range by mistake. It would be terribly embarrassing to
smash in John Q. Public's car while in the midst of a driver-training
program.

Examine the surface quality of your range. Are there soft spots?
Are there potholes that could damage or overturn a speeding car? *Be
cautious.*

TRAINING VEHICLES

Obviously, your training vehicles should be representative of police
vehicles. They should be in good mechanical condition. It's tempting
but don't single out the biggest lemons in your vehicle fleet and as-
sign them as training vehicles. Some police departments do this on
the pretense that the cars are going to be wrecked in training anyway, so why throw away perfectly good cars? *This is not a valid
excuse.* Driver training is not intended to show people how to smash
cars safely. It's intended to keep people from having accidents, not
how to get into them. The training cars should be:

1. Standard four-door cars representative of the type(s) used on
   the job.
2. Equipped with the large displacement engine required to ob-
   tain the needed speeds in a short distance. Again, train with
   equipment most like that used on the job.
3. Fitted with a heavy-duty or "special police package" suspension. These types of suspension generally require less maintenance.
4. Equipped with police pursuit tires inflated to manufacturer
   specifications. Proper tire pressure is stamped on the side of
   the tire. It is insanity to conduct an emergency driving course
   on second-rate tires. You might also consider overinflating the
   tires by no more than 5 lb above the manufacturer's maximum.
   This provides longer tire wear and a more controllable car under heavy loading.
5. Equipped with power steering.

6. As far as interior modifications, the use of roll bars on all police vehicles is strongly recommended. If you do opt for the installation of roll bars, you must also require students to wear helmets. To have roll bars and not wear a helmet is an invitation to smash one's head against the roll cage in an emergency.

In addition, all training cars should have:

- A fire extinguisher. *This is mandatory equipment!* The extinguisher should be well secured inside the vehicle, within easy reach of both trainee and instructor.
- Lap belts and shoulder harnesses. These are *mandatory* equipment for all vehicles.
- Two-way radios. Radios in each car are advisable for safety reasons and to ease the coordination of the exercise.

NECESSARY EQUIPMENT

Equipment required at the driving range includes the following:

- A first-aid kit equipped to handle minor injuries. Also, know the way to the closest hospital and, if possible, be in radio contact with the hospital.
- Approximately 125 to 140 orange safety cones, 12 inches to 14 inches tall. These are obstacle and replacement cones. Some 6-inch cones are useful for simulating the height of a curb.
- About 20 to 25 orange safety cones, 16 to 22 inches high, for use as key and obstacle-point cones. Be wary of cones larger than 22 inches; they can damage cars.
- A roller tape or standard 100-foot tape measure for marking off courses and setting up obstacles.
- Several different colors of spray paint. This is a must for laying out the course. Label the points on the ground where you will later put cones. You might try labeling them "S" for serpentine course, or "E" for evasive maneuver. The reason for several different colors isn't just to make the range a work of art. Color-coding will make everything much easier to find and you'll be able to set the range up quickly, with a minimum of wasted time. Use color to distinguish one type of course from another.

It could become dangerous and more than a little scary to drive onto a course that isn't the one a driver started out on.

- Extra fire extinguishers for the supply vehicle command post.
- Extra tires, wheels, and jacks.
- Perimeter markers and "Restricted Area" signs. These are helpful for securing the area.

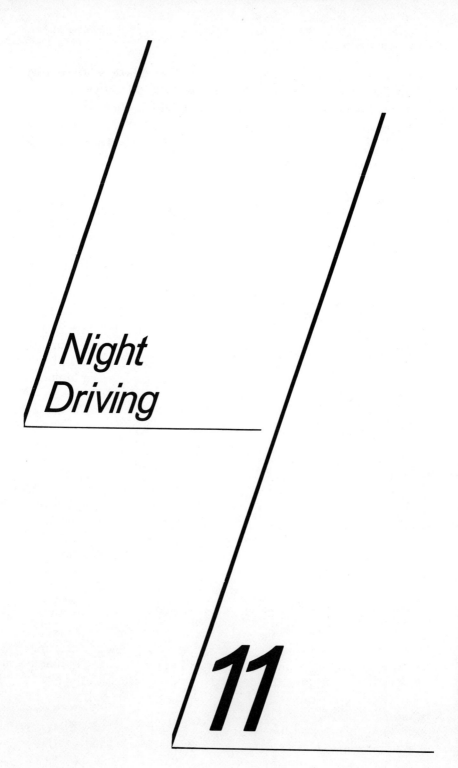

Night
Driving

11

Some police officers spend their entire duty shift driving in darkness and yet know very little about the fundamental differences between nighttime and daylight driving. But before we discuss the finer points of nocturnal navigation, let's take a close look at the amazing mechanism that makes all driving, whether by night or day, possible.

THE HUMAN EYE

This amazing mechanism is the human eye. But amazing or not, it does have a few shortcomings. Because humans did not evolve as true nocturnal animals, the human eye works far better in daylight than in reduced light conditions. Contrary to popular belief, low light does not impair the eye's ability to transmit visual data. The eye isn't any more or less adept at gathering light; it's just that we don't really see the physical world around us. What we see is light reflecting off the world around us. Light entering the eye is the source of the visual data we need, and when an insufficient amount of light enters the eye, the quality of the data transmitted to the brain suffers. The brain makes do with what it gets and presents the conscious mind with sometimes spotty results.

The eye detects and processes light in much the same way as a camera. Light enters the eye through the *pupil*, the round, dark opening at the front of the eye. The light then passes through a clear, lens-shaped membrane called the *cornea*. The cornea acts exactly like a lens, focusing and, to some degree, concentrating the light on a light-sensitive coating on the rear inner surface of the eye. This coating is called the *retina* and it's here that light is converted into nerve impulses that are transmitted to the brain for interpretation.

Two basic types of light-sensitive cells form the retina. Because of their shape, these cells are known as *rods* and *cones*. Rods are sensitive to low-level amounts of light energy; cones are sensitive to daylight intensities. It's mostly the rods that are at work when we drive at night.

Dusk and dawn are the two most difficult times of the day for good vision. In the changing light of dawn and dusk, the eye is caught in the middle, unable to rely either on rods or cones as the primary source of visual information. As the light fades and evening comes on, the rods gradually take over, and as the light conditions stabilize, your eyes adapt to the light and you are given the gift of night vision. Until that happens, and it happens each and every day, people run cars into one another in every imaginable way.

Police encounter some common transition problems between high-level and low-level light situations every day. For example, you're on night patrol, taking a meal break at a brightly illuminated truck stop. You receive an emergency call on your portable transceiver. You run out and jump into your cruiser. Remember, it takes time for the rods and cones to make the transition from high-level to low-level light. Thus, there will be a period of time when you cannot see very well.

It's the same when you walk into a movie house after the picture has already started. There you are in a darkened theater, probably juggling an armload of popcorn and soda, trying to find a seat you simply cannot see. You blunder into a seat, stepping on a few toes on the way, and after a few minutes, you notice how much more light the theater has. Your eyes have had the time they need to adapt to the new lighting situation. The older you get, the longer this adaptation process takes.

When the rods have taken over in very low-light situations, the pupil is dilated to permit more light to enter the eye. Unfortunately, the more dilated the pupil, the less efficient the eye, because, just like a camera lens, the eye loses *depth of field*. Depth of field is the range over which the eye is focused. In bright light, the pupil closes to protect the retina from too much light, and depth of field increases. When the pupil opens wide, depth of field decreases.

Near-sighted people in particular notice this effect, as do wearers of contact lenses, who discover that the diameter of their lenses provides insufficient peripheral coverage when the pupils are fully dilated.

At one time or another all of us have complained of tired eyes. But the eyes themselves do not tire. The nerves, brain, and body may fatigue and the heavy eyelids and burning sensation that most people associate with tired eyes are really the physical reactions of a tired body.

CAR DESIGN

Car design can affect night driving. Most cruisers are equipped with tinted glass, which helps keep the interior temperature low during sunny days, but also cuts visibility considerably in the dark of night.

The greenish or bluish tint of most instrument panel lights is bad for night vision. These colors are at the end of the spectrum to which the eye is least sensitive in low light. Some of the new cars from overseas and, lately, some built in the U.S. are equipped with red instrument lighting, a practice that's been common for quite some time in the aircraft industry. Red light does not interfere with vision outside of the car, and it makes the instruments much clearer to read. Red panel lighting eliminates the endless squinting down at the panel and the need for the eyes to continually readjust from glances at the instruments, or gazes at the road. This does much to reduce overall eye fatigue.

Although no figures are available as to whether red panel lighting has decreased accident rates, it does make long night drives more comfortable.

If you were eyeglasses and want to drive at peak efficiency at night, wear glasses with an antireflection (AR) coating on the lenses. The AR coating does much the same thing as similar coatings on binocular and camera lenses; it increases the lenses' efficiency by allowing them to transmit more light. At least 8 percent of the light is absorbed within a clear glass lens, but the same lens with an AR coating transmits 99 percent of the light.

Just because you must wear glasses does not mean there is anything radically wrong with your eyes. If your eye doctor says you must wear glasses, here are the specifications to ask for in the glasses you will use on the road:

- *Day:* Dark glasses. AR coating, gray-tinted lenses, sufficient lens coverage for peripheral vision, nonobstructive frames and temple pieces, lightweight, comfortable ear and nose pieces.
- *Night:* AR coating, yellow-tinted lenses. Same comfort specifications.
- *All-Around:* AR coating, slight cosmetic tint if required. Same comfort specifications.

Adding a yellow tint (for cosmetic purposes) will not reduce the light transmission characteristics of the lenses below 92 percent as long as the lenses are AR coated. The eye is most sensitive to the yellow portion of the spectrum, so yellow lenses are recommended for night use because they effectively increase the apparent viewing brilliance and alleviate 20 percent of usual night-driving fatigue. Yellow lenses also help on cloudy days, but the effect is usually too brilliant for sunny weather. Instead, gray lenses during the day provide the right amount of light while properly preparing our eyes for the coming darkness. After wearing gray lenses all day, your eyes will make the transition to reduced light levels much more readily, and what you see will be a much more accurate picture of what's really happening after dark.

Recently some dramatic discoveries were made about sunglasses. It seems that the amount of light your eyes take in during the day is a factor in how well you see at night. This means you should always wear sunglasses when driving during daylight hours. And make sure those are good-quality sunglasses. Buy them with consideration toward how well they'll treat your eyes and not toward how good they look on you.

Corning Glass has developed a line of sunglasses especially designed for driving. Called "Serengeti Drivers," these sunglasses are specifically designed to filter out the harmful daylight rays that affect how we see at night. To our knowledge, these are the only commercially available sunglasses that perform this function. Serengeti Drivers have been tested by police officers and received many favorable reviews.

NIGHT DRIVING

But enough about eyes and eye protection. Let's talk about the actual task of operating a motor vehicle at night. Night operations are probably the least understood aspects of driving. Most drivers, police included, think the only major difference between day and night driving is that one requires the use of headlights.

The first major, and startling, difference between day and night driving is the accident rate. The night-driving accident rate is truly appalling, roughly three times that of daylight driving. This high accident rate is the result of much more than simply driving when it's dark. Other factors, such as alcohol and drug abuse and driver fatigue, enter into the nocturnal accident equation. But poor visibility is a part of the big picture. At night, the driver's normally wide field of vision is narrowed to the field of view illuminated by your headlights, the headlights of other vehicles, and fixed road lights.

When viewed at night, most objects exhibit relatively low contrast, which makes their detection, especially against certain backgrounds, extremely difficult. Colors fade at night. Peripheral vision is decreased. Plainly said, it's hard to see at night.

Contrary to common sense, most drivers do not slow down significantly when driving at night, despite their reduced visibility and the added dangers of inclement weather. We've all seen this type of driver. You're tooling along at a reduced speed at night in a driving rainstorm. The windshield wipers are slapping back and forth at their highest setting when suddenly a pair of headlights appear in your rearview mirror. These headlights grow bigger and brighter at an alarming rate and before we know it—zoom!—a car goes flashing past us, apparently oblivious to the darkness, the weather, and the fact that it's hard to see 50 feet ahead of the car on a night like this. This driver is doing what is known as overdriving the headlights.

Headlights

Most of the light we have available for our use at night comes from our car's headlights. Except for our speedy and foolhardy friend above, we can only drive as fast as our eyes can see. An example will illustrate:

It's night and you're driving with your low-beam headlights on, which permit you to see about 200 feet ahead of you. If your speed is 40 mph (approximately 60 ft/sec) you have three seconds' worth of vision ahead of you, assuming that your headlights are clean and working at maximum efficiency.

Sadly, one of the most dangerous aspects of night driving is one that we can little control: blinding glare from oncoming headlights. Much research has been conducted into the problems of glare and night vision, and all these studies have reached the same startling conclusion: *When your eyes are hit by a bright beam of light from an oncoming car, you can't see!*

How much is vision impaired by this type of attack? We can be completely blinded for a full one or two seconds, which means that at 40 mph you will drive somewhere from 60 to 120 feet without being able to see anything clearly.

Drivers can be affected by the oncoming glare of headlights as far as 3,000 feet away. If you feel you won't be able to see after a car approaching you has passed, slow down and try not to look directly at the oncoming headlights. Looking at the right side of the road is often effective.

Bright color and high contrast make objects visible at night. That's why it's a good idea to have some reflecting tape on the outside of your vehicle, especially if the vehicle is a dark color.

Good night visibility is more than just having headlights. Equally important is the alignment of those lights. You can have the best headlight system in the world, but if those lights point off in crazy directions, they're not going to do much good, except to make your vehicle a kind of traveling light show. Tests can be performed to see if the lights on your department's cruisers are aligned properly.

It's important also to keep headlights clean. As much as half of a headlight's total illumination can be absorbed by dirt on the surface of the glass beam. Keeping headlights clean is especially important in winter when they are frequently covered with road dirt and encrusted with salt.

Headlights cannot see around corners. They light only the path of travel that is straight ahead. When we do turn corners at night, we tend to follow the headlights around that corner. When you turn your car, scan the areas to the side and beyond the headlights. Also, when backing up, remember that only your backup lights are available; on most makes of cars, they aren't much. There's not much more you can do but cope with this reality.

Windshields

A clean windshield is vital for driving whether in day or night. Streaks and smears on windshields can produce extremely disorienting kaleidoscopic effects when lights shine on them at night. Make sure your windshield washers work, that your windshield wiper blades are clean and not old and worn out, and that the windshield wiper fluid container is kept filled.

Keeping the inside of the windshield clean is equally important. If you smoke or drive with someone who does, clean the inside of the windshield every other day. It's amazing how fast smoke residue builds up on the inside of a car's windshield.

Finally, here are some rules to help minimize the hazards of night driving:

1. *Adjust your speed to the range of your headlights.* High-beam headlights in good working order illuminate the road for about 330 feet ahead; low beams illuminate for a much shorter distance (Fig. 11-1). Accordingly, adjust the two-second rule for traffic ahead of you to a three-second rule. Don't overdrive your headlights.

2. *Keep your eyes moving.* Don't fall for the temptation of focusing on the middle of the lighted area in front of you. Search the edges of the lighted area. Look for other patches of light that could be cars. Look for them at hilltops, on curves, or at intersections. Where there are many distracting neon signs or brightly lit buildings, try to concentrate on street-level activities.

3. *Protect your eyes from glare.* Prolonged exposure to glare from sunlight during the day or headlights at night can temporarily ruin your night vision, while also leading to eye strain and drowsiness. Wear good sunglasses on bright days and take them off as

Night Driving

1. Measure night blindness.
2. Understand how you can overdrive your lights.
3. Become aware of peripheral vision problems at night.
4. Learn to drive within your limits.

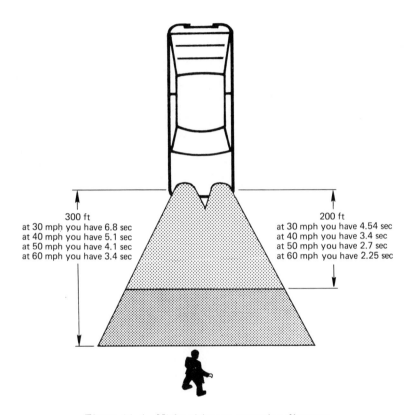

300 ft
at 30 mph you have 6.8 sec
at 40 mph you have 5.1 sec
at 50 mph you have 4.1 sec
at 60 mph you have 3.4 sec

200 ft
at 30 mph you have 4.54 sec
at 40 mph you have 3.4 sec
at 50 mph you have 2.7 sec
at 60 mph you have 2.25 sec

Figure 11-1   Night vision vs. stopping distance.

soon as the sun goes down. Rest a while before driving at night after a long session of steady daytime driving.

4. *Keep windshields and headlights clean.*

5. *Use your lights wisely.* Use high beams when possible. Switch to low beams when following another car or encountering oncoming cars. Flash your lights as a signal when overtaking and passing.

6. *Make it easy for others to see you.* Turn on your low beams at dusk or dawn. Used at this time of day, they won't help you

see but they'll help other drivers and pedestrians see you. If
you have to pull off the road and stop, for whatever reason, put
on your emergency flashers. It's not a bad idea to turn on the
car's interior or dome lights. If the car's electrical system fails,
have a combination of flares, a flashlight, and some reflective
materials handy.

7. *Avoid steady driving at the hour of your usual bedtime.* A person's alertness level decreases around the time one routinely
retires for the night. If you must drive past your usual bedtime,
stop every hour or so and walk around. Stretch your legs. Get
some air.

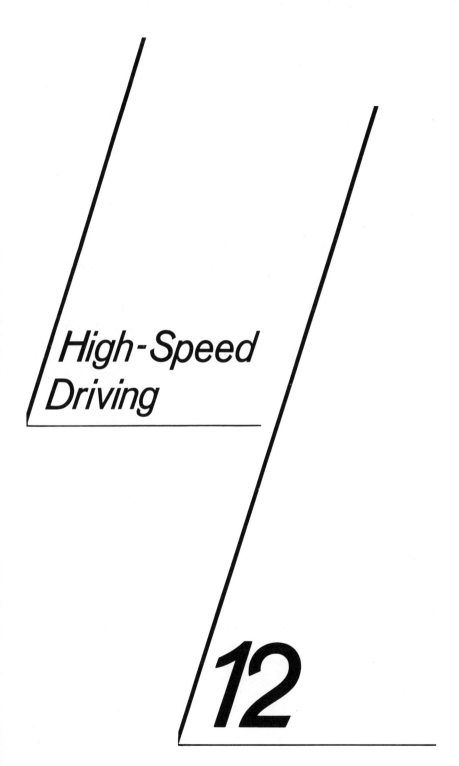

High-Speed Driving

12

The real world of police driving is made up of countless hours of boredom, punctuated by a few minutes of driving on the wild side. Many people, including some administrators, say that driving fast is bad for you, that it will eventually make you go blind, or some such nonsense. But the plain truth is that high-performance driving is a lot of fun. It can really get the adrenaline pumping, and adrenaline can be very habit-forming.

When examining the entire issue of high-speed driving seriously and soberly, a single fact emerges. There is only one reason for you, as a police officer, to drive fast and that's in response to an emergency call.

Long-term highway cruising at high speed tends to become hypnotic and can make you forget why you started driving fast in the first place. All of us have had the experience of driving down a smooth, straight freeway only to glance down at the speedometer and discover ourselves driving far faster than we thought we were, and well over the posted speed limit. Upon our discovery, we immediately slow to a legal speed, only to feel as if we were crawling down the road, even though still moving at a good clip. Our minds and reflexes have been accelerated by the high-speed rush and take much longer to slow down than the car we're driving.

Remember: Speed is addictive and can play tricks with your mind. Speed can lure you into situations you can't get out of. Driving fast can be fun, but it's dangerous. Don't ever forget that. Treat speed with the respect it deserves, but don't be afraid of it.

SKILL REQUIRED

You were not born with the skills needed for high-speed driving. Just because you can handle your vehicle skillfully and safely in everyday traffic doesn't mean you can do what needs to be done at high speed. A great deal of skill is required to drive fast. There's no shame to admitting that high-speed driving is something you're not especially good at. Just because you play a pretty good game of softball with the department team doesn't mean that you're ready for the major leagues. Just as there's no comparison between the sandlot leagues and the big time, there's no comparison between routine driving and driving fast.

It's the same when comparing driving a police cruiser with driving a Formula I race car. It's comparing apples and oranges; one is completely different from the other. And we don't mean to imply that driving the racing car is any more dangerous or requires any more nerve than everyday police work. Most race drivers admit they would not like to drive the way police do, in an uncontrolled environment, surrounded by cars piloted by other drivers with completely different skill levels, many of them marginally competent at best. Racing drivers drive fast in a far different driving environment: on enclosed raceways, with all the cars traveling the same direction, no intersections, no traffic lights, no pedestrians, and everyone in possession of roughly the same level of skill.

The best advice to you as an emergency driver is to *drive smart*, not fast. Driving smart will get you where you need to go. Driving fast, this is not always true.

The speeds you drive should be within the policy guidelines set down by your department. As a police officer, you must know what those guidelines are. Perhaps you disagree with the rules, but you'd better abide by them because in the event of an accident, if you are found to have violated those rules, you'll be the party held accountable and you'll suffer the consequences, which can be devastating.

ODDS OF AN ACCIDENT

If you get into a collision at 75 mph, you are more than likely going to suffer a serious disabling injury—or worse. The chances of being killed in an accident at that speed are one in eight.

At 65 mph, there is a one in 20 chance of dying in an accident at that speed. At 55 mph, the chances are one in 50.

These are not great odds. Let's take a look at some of the things that happen when you drive fast. The first is the effect speed has on peripheral vision (Fig. 12-1). An average person with good peripheral vision can see about 180 degrees from side to side when the vehicle is stationary. Traveling at 40 mph, a driver's peripheral vision is cut to 120 degrees; at 50 mph peripheral vision is reduced to 90 degrees; at 60 mph it goes down to 60 degrees; at 80 mph peripheral vision amounts to a mere 30 degrees.

Loss of Peripheral Vision

How many times have you heard collision survivors say, "I just didn't see the other car"? Often they're correct; they really didn't see the other car because of this loss of peripheral vision. This explains how drivers can cruise right through intersections, narrowly missing cars they never ever saw.

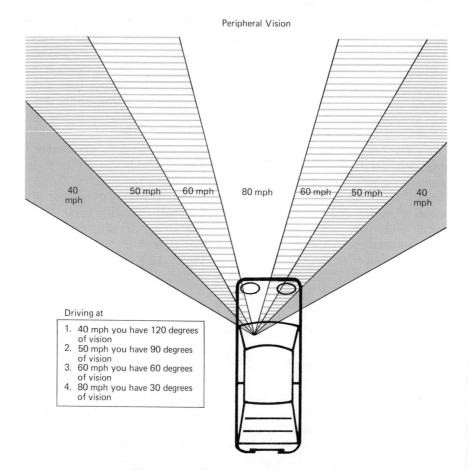

Peripheral Vision

Driving at
1. 40 mph you have 120 degrees of vision
2. 50 mph you have 90 degrees of vision
3. 60 mph you have 60 degrees of vision
4. 80 mph you have 30 degrees of vision

Figure 12-1   Peripheral vision vs. speed.

As we've already indicated, the greatest danger from this loss of peripheral vision occurs at higher speeds. At 80 mph, peripheral vision is reduced to the point where you won't see a vehicle approaching at a 90-degree angle from either side until that vehicle is in the front seat with you. Keep these numbers in mind the next time you decide to pursue a car at 50 mph through a neighborhood with a lot of side streets. At those speeds, it's like driving with blinders on. To prevent accidents, you've got to be able to see them first. The way to spot conflicting traffic is to scan every intersection, every opening of every side street, before proceeding into the intersection. At high speeds, this is going to mean a lot of eye movement, but at high speeds, virtually every other part of your nervous system is working at maximum speeds. Why shouldn't your eyes pitch in and help?

If you have a partner, have the partner supplement your peripheral vision by double-checking intersections and serving as your second set of eyes. At high speeds, you must know what's going on around you. What you don't know can prove disastrous. Be aware of your environment.

KINETIC ENERGY

As we know, the higher the car's speed, the more distance required to stop. A look at the processes involved in stopping a car reveals much about the forces acting on that car when we try to stop it and relates those forces to speed. The most important force we're dealing with in stopping is *kinetic energy*. This is the energy stored in bodies in motion. Kinetic energy can be expressed in an equation:

$$K.E. = WV^2/2(G)$$

where K.E. = Kinetic energy
 W = Weight of the car
 V = Car's velocity in ft/sec.
 G = Force of gravity (32.2), otherwise known as the gravitational constant

As with our previous equations, whereas it's important to understand both the practical implications of and theoretical roots of each equation, it's not necessary to memorize each one.

Using the above equation it's possible to compute that if a 4,000-lb car traveling 60 mph must be stopped, a way has to be found to dissipate about 525,000 ft/lb of energy. That's the equivalent of lifting 262 tons one foot off the ground (Fig. 12-2).

Kinetic energy increases dramatically with speed. Some drivers think there's something magical about stopping a car, but the basic physical principles are quite simple. To stop, a way to eliminate all the kinetic energy stored in the moving car must be found. The way to do this is to apply the car's brakes, thereby transforming the kinetic energy in the moving car into heat when the brakes are applied.

These basic principles hold true for everyone. There are no exceptions, no special cases. No matter how good a driver you are, it takes twice as long and four times as much distance to stop a car going 60 mph compared to one that's traveling at 30 mph. You have no control over this.

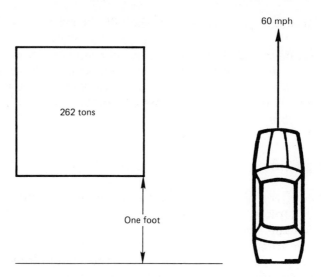

Figure 12-2 Kinetic energy and speed. At 60 mph a car has developed enough energy to lift 262 tons one foot off the ground.

As if stopping weren't difficult enough, we also have to recognize and manage the forces at work on the vehicle in a turn. As we've learned, every time you turn the steering wheel, inertial and centrifugal forces work on the vehicle, pushing it to the outside of the turn. The strength of these forces is determined by speed; the faster you drive, the more force is placed on the vehicle. At some point, the force overwhelms the vehicle and pushes it right off the road.

You can drive a given corner every day on patrol and think you know it well. Yet take that corner at high speed and it will be like driving around it for the very first time. Cars corner very differently at different speeds. To make matters worse, speed is not the only consideration you have in taking corners fast. The car's position on the road is as important as its speed.

To better understand positioning, review Chapter 7 on cornering techniques. It is vital to your safety and the safety of others for you to learn to drive corners by taking the proper line and apex.

Leaving the Ground

Speed exaggerates flaws in the road. What feels like a little bump at 35 mph can be a launching ramp at 60 mph. Road obstacles such as railroad crossings can send a car flying through the air. In one such instance, an officer was killed because his cruiser hit a bump at high speed, was launched into the air and collided with a tree. The point of impact was *five feet off the ground!*

If you do happen to become airborne because of a high-speed encounter with a rut, bump, or railroad crossing, *do not* move the steering wheel while the vehicle is in the air. Because the front wheels are not touching the ground, turning the steering wheel accomplishes nothing. In fact, moving the wheel can spell disaster. If you turn the wheel while airborne, the car's front wheels will be turned in relation to the path of the car before it took off. If the wheels have been turned, the car could go off the road upon touching down. If the front wheels have been turned drastically, the car could cartwheel or roll. If for any reason you become airborne, hang on, keep the wheels pointed straight ahead, and hope for the best when you land.

Smoothness of control operation at high speeds is a must. As speeds increase, the car becomes an extremely sensitive instrument; a slight movement of the controls can cause the car to become unstable. A rough movement of the steering wheel at 75 mph can send you hurtling off the road in milliseconds.

Braking.   The same is true for brakes. When approaching a corner at high speed, don't try to brake and turn at the same time. You will overload the front tires, pushing them past their limits of adhesion, and then go out of control. Slow down on approach to the curve and then turn the wheel.

Becoming fixated.   As stated previously, as speed increases, peripheral vision decreases. As speed increases, a driver's eyes tend to focus on objects just a short distance in front of the car's hood. This is ironic. Common sense says that the faster you drive the farther ahead of the car your attention should be focused. After all, the reason you're driving fast in the first place is that you are in a pursuit situation, which means you're probably fixing your eyes on the vehicle you're chasing. That raises a couple of problems. If you're completely fixated on the vehicle you're chasing, then you're probably doing with your vehicle what the other driver is doing with his or her vehicle. If the driver being pursued takes a corner using the wrong line and apex, you're likely to do the same thing. In fact, you're likely to repeat any of the mistakes the other driver makes. Obviously, this is wrong, because what you're trying to do is catch that car, not pace it. To do that, you have to drive better than the person you are chasing.

As we stated at the outset, high-speed driving is addictive. When the adrenaline flows in a high-speed chase, you tend to do things you would not ordinarily do. Fatigue seems to exaggerate this tendency, so much so that the worst thing you could probably do with a vehicle is enter into a high-speed chase while tired, because you're likely to do some pretty crazy things.

THE FEAR FACTOR

How fast you do drive should be governed by the "Fear Factor." The Fear Factor is something none of us like to talk about. (It can be your little secret—you don't have to tell your fellow officers that you have one. You don't want to tell them about yours because then they'll have to tell you about theirs.)

Being the proud owner of a Fear Factor is a very healthy thing, and it is nothing to be ashamed of because the Fear Factor keeps you alive. Don't try to fight your Fear Factor. If you're driving at a speed that makes you want to throw up, that's both God and the Fear Factor telling you to slow down.

Your partner is also a good judge of how fast you should be driving. If your partner is turning various shades of green and otherwise indicating to you that the speed you are driving is not particularly appreciated, heed your partner's warning. In such a case, your partner's Fear Factor is taking over where yours left off, and two Fear Factors are better than one.

If fear is not an adequate motivator, think of your family. Ask yourself the question, "What would happen if I went off the road at this speed?" If the answer bothers you, slow down.

The faster you drive, the more often you should consult your speedometer. You cannot rely on your own judgment; the faster you drive, the more your perception of speed becomes distorted. This is why people in court testifying in an accident case cannot remember how fast they were going when the accident occurred. They truly have no idea how fast they were moving. But when police officers get up in court and respond "I don't know" when asked the speed of their cruiser when it hit those six parked cars in the church parking lot, those officers are in real trouble.

Bear in mind that the faster you drive, the more passing you'll have to do. In fact, you will find yourself driving in lanes designated for oncoming traffic much more often than you'd like to. Passing is dangerous to begin with but can be devastating when done fast.

WEATHER

Weather, always an important factor, is even more important during high-speed driving. Driving fast in the rain is extremely dangerous. If you encounter a large puddle while driving fast, you will definitely hydroplane; that is, your tires will ride up on a cushion of water. This water cushion can be slicker than ice, leaving you with no control. It's very easy to go off the road while hydroplaning. If you feel the vehicle begin to hydroplane (the effect usually begins with the front wheels) *do not hit the brakes.* The same general rules for icy surfaces apply here: Back off the power, maintain as straight a path as possible, and you should soon feel control returning to you (Fig. 12-3).

The three conditions that result in chronic hydroplaning are (1) a heavy rain that either creates large puddles or falls on a road with poor drainage, so that the rain coats the entire road surface in a fairly uniform sheet, (2) a vehicle with worn tires, and (3) speed in excess of 50 mph.

Here are some basic rules to follow in high-speed situations:

1. Don't drive faster than you can see.
2. Driving fast is a skill that cannot be learned by driving slowly. Just because you are a competent slow-speed driver, do not assume the same will hold true at higher speeds. Training, practice, and experience are needed to become a competent high-speed driver.
3. When you increase speed, you are suddenly driving a very different car from the one you were in control of a few moments

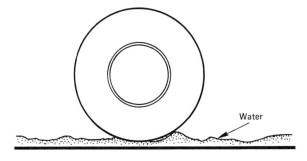

Figure 12-3 Tires and hydroplaning. Heavy rains + speeds of over 50 mph + worn tires = a lot of pain.

ago. When speed is increased from 20 mph to 60 mph, the speed of the vehicle has been tripled but the amount of distance required to stop has been increased nine times. Turning the steering wheel at 60 mph will put nine times as much stress on the car as the same maneuver at 20 mph. A car's controls are extremely sensitive to speed; the faster you go, the more sensitive they become.

4. Remember: There's nothing worth losing your life over, especially a high-speed pursuit.

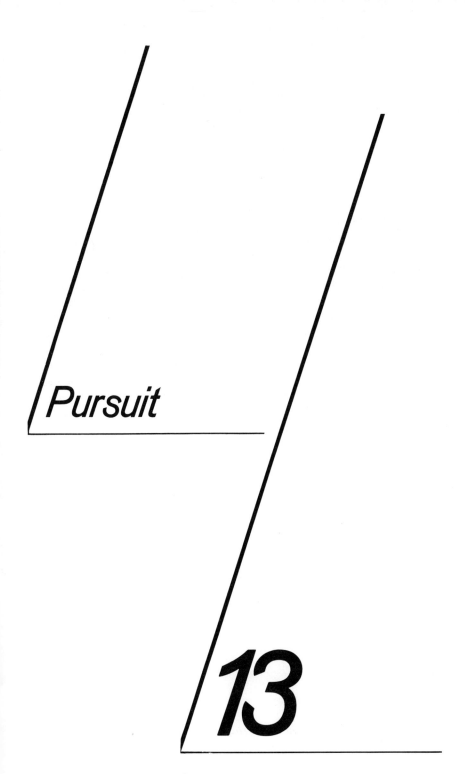

Pursuit

13

Once you initiate a pursuit, there's no way you can win at it. You can only lose. That may sound rather negative but it's the truth.

You could spot a most-wanted fugitive tooling around town in a car, give chase, do a great job of driving, apprehend the suspect, perform the arrest procedures so everything is iron-clad and legal. There is no way of this individual getting off with a clever lawyer and a convenient technicality. Your colleagues will pat you on the back, tell you what a great job you did, and buy you a beer. More than likely the public will collectively yawn, say "Ho-hum, that's what you get paid to do," and go back to sleep.

However, make a mistake in that same pursuit, especially a mistake that causes injury or death to an innocent third party, and the entire world will come down around your ears. Suddenly a hidden clause emerges in the unwritten contract that you, as a police officer, have with society. In that contract, you agree to apprehend those individuals society deems as criminals. The hidden clause asks at what cost these apprehensions take place. How many smashed cars or injured bystanders are worth catching a murderer? It's an open-ended clause because there's no agreement on whether police pursuits are worth the potential danger to life and property. This is a constant ground for controversy between police officials and the public. And it's an important controversy. High-speed police chases are a serious matter, one that demands the same amount of attention as questions on the use of deadly force. Driving a 4,000-lb vehicle at speeds well above the speed limit is plainly and simply a potential use of deadly force (Fig. 13-1).

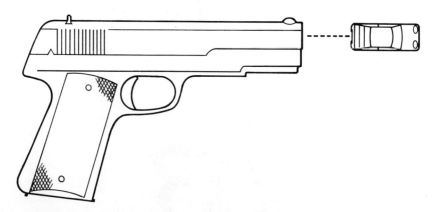

Figure 13-1 Vehicles and deadly force. Use of deadly force: Driving a car is as deadly as shooting a gun.

RESEARCH FINDINGS

It's amazing that such a complex and potentially deadly problem has not received more attention in the form of scientific research. Rather, the subject of high-speed pursuit has been reduced to groundless speculation. But some research, albeit not very timely, has been undertaken on the issue of high-speed chases. In 1970, a U.S. Department of Labor study presented the following findings:

- Each year between 50,000 and 500,000 "hot" pursuits occur in the U.S.
- 6,000 to 8,000 of these pursuits resulted in crashes.
- 300 to 400 people were killed in these crashes.
- 2,500 to 5,000 people were injured in these crashes.

The California Highway Patrol conducted a six-month survey in which it studied 683 police pursuits. Findings showed a one in three chance that a pursuit will end in an accident, a 10 percent chance that someone will be injured in that collision, and a 1 percent chance that someone will be killed.

The lack of solid research data overall does not conceal the fact that high-speed pursuits are a serious police concern. The administrative problems caused by collisions alone are consequential. A great deal has been written about the havoc they cause, and about the pain and suffering of a chase with a fatal outcome. Nothing justifies an innocent third party being injured in a chase. This author has no intention of denigrating or disregarding the grief caused by pursuit accidents.

TO PURSUE OR NOT TO PURSUE

What we do want to talk about are the problems police have with this sensitive subject. In a high-speed pursuit situation, the officer has to make a snap decision, to pursue or not to pursue. Then the chase takes place, in what are probably impossible conditions, where many things can go wrong, and if and when something does go wrong, the officer pays for it, sometimes through loss of the officer's own life and/or limbs.

Pursuit is a two-sided coin. On one side we have the attorney for the two adolescents killed driving a stolen car while a police cruiser was chasing them. The attorney says, "I don't think police should be allowed to chase cars at high speed through crowded city streets just for the sake of recovering a stolen car. Cars can be replaced but lives cannot."

From the viewpoint of many law-enforcement professionals, lawbreakers cannot be simply let off the hook if they know that all they have to do is climb into a car and drive fast through crowded city streets to evade capture, secure in the knowledge that the police will not chase them.

Imagine yourself a civilian driver, minding his or her own business, sitting in one's car at an intersection, waiting to make a turn. There is a police cruiser directly behind you. Your turn comes. You've got the right of way. Just as you're about to proceed into the intersection, a driver from your right streaks through the intersection, runs the stop sign, and very nearly plows into you. What would you think if the officer in that police car failed to pursue the vehicle that ran that stop sign? What would you think if the officer in that patrol car just remained behind you, doing nothing?

On the other hand, what if the officer did decide to pursue the car that ran the stop sign, but instead of being in traffic in front of the patrol car, this time you were at another intersection a few miles down the road. You're driving across the road when suddenly the fleeing vehicle slams into your car. Would you still say that this particular high-speed chase was worth it? We rather doubt it.

Deputy Superintendent Robert O'Toole, driving trainer for the Boston Police Academy, puts it in perspective when he says, "Everyone says they've got a better way. Well, if you can think of one, please let us know."

The following is intended to help two groups of people: those who write police department pursuit policies and those in the front seats of their cruisers who are trying to adhere to those policies and still get the job done. Here are some points to keep in mind:

1. *When to initiate pursuit:* Probably the most important issue.
2. *The maximum number of police units permitted in a pursuit:* You do not want an 80-mph police parade through your city.
3. *Responsibilities of the primary and secondary units:* Should be carefully delineated ahead of time.
4. *Driving tactics:* Know what you can and cannot do.
5. *Communications:* Let everyone know what you're doing. Ideally, your partner should handle the radio chores while you concentrate on driving.
6. *Capture:* Always keep in mind just what you're going to do

once you catch up with your quarry and the individual does not pull over.

7. *Discontinuance of pursuit:* Under what conditions the pursuit is no longer worth it.
8. *Supervisory responsibilities:* Who's in charge of a multivehicle pursuit?
9. *Firearms use:* When appropriate. But never fire a weapon from a moving vehicle. Leave that for the movies.
10. *Blocking tactics:* Ramming, boxing, roadblocks.
11. *Absolute speed limits:* Just how far will you go?
12. *Interjurisdictional considerations:* When have you exceeded your jurisdiction? Who takes over when you have exceeded it?
13. *Overall conditions:* Vehicles, drivers, roadway, weather, traffic.
14. *Hazards to other users of the highway.*
15. *Reporting procedures and postpursuit analysis.*

The U.S. Department of Transportation offers guidelines on high-speed pursuit that cover emergency vehicle authorization. The guidelines read as follows:

(a) The driver of an authorized emergency vehicle, when responding to an emergency call or when in the pursuit of an actual or suspected violator of the law and when responding to but not upon returning from a fire alarm, may exercise the privileges set forth in this section, but subject to the condition herein stated.
(b) The driver of the authorized emergency vehicle may:
  1. Park or stand, irrespective of the provisions of this chapter.
  2. Proceed past a red or stop signal or stop sign, but only after slowing down as necessary for safe operation.
  3. Exceed the maximum speed limits so long as he or she does not endanger life or property.
  4. Disregard regulations governing direction of movement or turning in specified directions.
(c) The exemption herein granted to an authorized emergency vehicle shall apply only when such a vehicle is making use of an audible signal meeting the requirements of Section 12-401(d) and visual signals meeting the requirements of Section 12-218 of this act, except that an authorized emergency vehicle operated as a police vehicle need not be equipped with or display a red light visible from in front of the vehicle.

(d) The foregoing provisions shall not relieve the driver of an authorized emergency vehicle from the duty to drive with due regard
for the safety of all persons, nor shall such provisions protect
the driver from the consequences of his reckless disregard for
the safety of others.

Section A of the guidelines states that an officer pursues "an actual or suspected violator of the law." The question is, how does the
driver know if the person being chased is a suspected felon? All pursuit accidents are measured with hindsight. All the Monday morning
quarterbacks will be telling you what you should have done. The
decision to pursue or not to pursue is a judgment call that is entirely
dependent on the pursuing officer(s).

Section B of the guidelines grants permission to exceed speed
limits but cautions that the driver cannot endanger life or property.
This is an extremely gray area because it is very difficult to exceed
the speed limit without endangering life or property. That's why
speed limits are posted in the first place. This regulation is essentially
a contradiction in terms, and once more demands a judgment call
from the officer(s).

Section C of the guidelines mentions that the driver is permitted
to drive through stop signs and exceed speed limits in pursuit only
when:

1. Meeting the requirements of Section 12-401(d) of the Uniform
   Vehicle Code. Under Section 12-401(d) the police siren must
   have a siren audible from a distance not less than 500 ft. The
   siren must also be activated on a continuous basis throughout
   the pursuit, or high speed chase. Even with this provision, the
   officer must remember that there are limitations on the capabilities of a siren to effectively warn all roadway users away
   from the approach of an emergency vehicle. Should a driver
   obviously not realize that an emergency vehicle was approaching and an accident appears probable, it is the officer's duty to
   avoid the collision.

2. The police unit must be capable of visually alerting traffic of
   its approach. This is done through utilization of the unit's overhead emergency lights (blue or red, or a combination, depending on the state's policy) throughout the entire chase, from the
   initial attempt to make the traffic stop until the completion or
   termination of the pursuit.

Section D of the guidelines mentions the driver must have "due regard for safety of all persons." The bottom line is simple. No matter how many carefully worded regulations governments and police departments write, the decision to pursue or not to pursue is a judgment call left to the police officer.

EMERGENCIES

Let's get down to the basics. What's an emergency? Well, emergencies include:

- Officer in need of assistance
- Hold-up in progress
- Explosion
- Scene-to-hospital transportation
- Person has swallowed poison; is burned; is in shock; is afflicted with uncontrolled arterial bleeding; has multiple injuries.
- An area-wide emergency status has been declared.

What's high speed? High speed is easy to define but difficult to quantify. Generally, what is considered high speed is 70 mph by municipal police departments and 85 mph by county and state police departments.

Speed limits pose a problem, namely, what is fast? Fast and dangerous driving could be going through a 20 mph zone at 35 mph. Slow could be 50 mph on a divided highway. A police officer in a high-speed chase at 70 mph through a downtown business district at noon of a Saturday is driving fast and bordering on insanity.

If the aftermath of a high-speed pursuit takes place in a courtroom, one of the important points about the case will be determining the officer's average speed during the pursuit. The lawyer for the plaintiff (those bringing suit against you and your department) is going to try to convince the judge and/or jury that you were driving like a maniac with total disregard to everyone else. If you can prove that your average speed throughout the pursuit was nowhere near as high as the lawyer claims, you may be able to discredit the lawyer's charge. Sound difficult? It isn't as tough as it sounds.

Determining average speed can be accomplished by developing a system between the departmental dispatcher and the pursuing officer. This system requires the dispatcher to record times to the

second. If the pursuing officer reports the beginning of the pursuit
to the dispatcher, the dispatcher can record it. The record should be
as precise as possible. Say an officer reports a pursuit beginning at
3:14:56 A.M. The dispatcher notes this on a log. Minutes later, the
pursuing officer radios a position report at the Dunkin' Donuts at
Third and Main at 3:16:10 A.M. Then, at 3:18:58, the officer has to
report "There's been an accident involving a third party . . ." and
gives a location and time.

These time references, when compared to a map of the area, can
accurately and irrefutably provide a speed record of the pursuit. In
this pursuit, the total time elapsed was four minutes and two seconds, or 242 seconds. If the measured distance of the pursuit is, say,
5.3 miles, then the distance traveled was 27,984 feet (5.3 mi $\times$ 5,280
ft). That averages out to 115.6 ft/sec. To convert ft/sec into mph,
divide by 1.47; therefore, the cruiser's average speed was 115.6 $\div$
1.47 = 78.7 mph.

With precise records, times, and locations such as these, the laws
of physics are pretty hard to argue against in court.

WHEN TO SAY NO

As difficult as deciding when to pursue is deciding when the risk is
no longer worth it and the pursuit should be aborted. The worst
thing you can do is let the pursuit become a personal challenge to
your ego, in other words, a vendetta. Ego is important to your job,
but don't let it get the best of you in a pursuit.

You should consider abandoning a pursuit when:

- The speeds are getting beyond the limit of you and your vehicle.
- You are exposing innocent bystanders to unnecessary danger.
- Weather conditions do not allow for the maximum use of your
  vehicle's abilities.
- The car you're pursuing shows no sign of stopping, even when
  and if you do catch up with it.

At a recent police seminar, a film was shown of an actual pursuit. Included in the film was aerial footage that showed one of the
police cruisers actually ramming the pursued car. Every time the
cruiser rammed its target, a big cheer arose from the audience.

In a pursuit, this sort of frustration can build to the point where
you will do anything to get that other car off the road. You'll do

anything to make the driver stop, for both the driver's own sake and the sake of the people you have sworn to protect. *Don't let this happen to you.* If the car you're pursuing won't pull over, *don't try to push the vehicle off the road.* Drop back a safe distance and wear out the fleeing driver. You've got the car to do it with. Eventually the speeding driver will either crash, tire and stop, or simply run out of gas and give up.

Back at that cheering seminar, I wonder what would have happened to those cheers if the film showed the pursued vehicle driving off the road and injuring several children.

SIRENS

Even though you have your lights and siren on, you cannot expect traffic to part as if it were the Red Sea (Fig. 13-2). Remember: Most people don't hear the siren in time to react to it. And when they finally do react, their reactions can be bizarre. A test conducted for the U.S. Department of Transportation investigating the effectiveness of sirens indicated the severe limitations of those devices. For

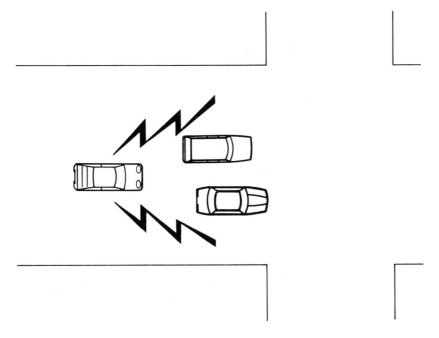

Figure 13-2 Sirens in traffic. Cars will not get out of your way.

pedestrians, sirens are effective in open areas. About 91 percent of the pedestrians tested could tell where the siren noise was coming from. When people were tested in a closed car, with the windows rolled up, only 26 percent could tell which direction the siren sound was coming from.

This means that in traffic situations, the siren is not a reliable directional indicator. Distance effectiveness deteriorated remarkably too. Under ideal traffic test conditions, the maximum distance the siren was audible was 440 feet, but when all the test subjects' scores were compared, the average distance came to just 125 feet. At 50 mph, the best-case scenario would give you six seconds' worth of warning, and under worst conditions, you'd have barely two seconds of warning time.

Perhaps six seconds is enough time to react, but two seconds certainly isn't (Fig. 13-3). Therefore, when on an emergency call, you should assume that no one can really hear your siren and proceed on that assumption. Assume people can't hear it and if they can, that they have no idea from which direction it's approaching.

Given this assumption, you should approach intersections with extreme caution in a pursuit. Don't go screaming into the intersection and assume that everyone there will know exactly what to do and where to go. Life does not work that way.

There will always be a lot of people wanting to go the way you are going. It's not that you're that popular; it's not that you're a

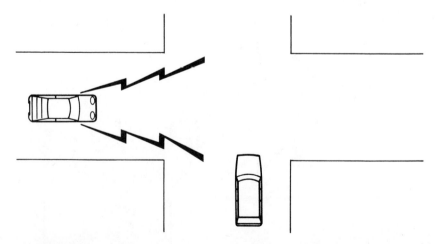

Figure 13-3 Time required to react to a siren. At 50 mph a car may have six seconds to react to your siren, but more than likely only two seconds.

trendsetter. It's a phenomenon called traffic. If you are blocked by traffic, you will suddenly find that your bright flashing lights and shrieking siren are not magic. They cannot make traffic disappear. In fact, the siren can make matters worse. The minds of many people tend to freeze up when confronted with a screaming siren mounted atop a police car that fills their rearview mirror. These people just succumb to a sort of paralysis and find they cannot move. In such a case, it's probably better for you to lay off the siren until the traffic starts to sort itself out. Here, as in most other aspects of the pursuit mission, if a driver panics and plows into another car because your siren unnerved that individual, guess who's going to stare down the wrong end of a lawsuit?

ATTITUDE

The officer's overall attitude during a pursuit is very important. Pursuit should be based on the driver's skill in controlling the car in the particular environment one happens to be in at the time, along with the type of vehicle one is driving. If the environment is a crowded city street at noon, perhaps the whole matter of a pursuit should be questioned. If you let your emotions get the better of you in a pursuit, you're just an accident looking for a place to happen. And it may be an accident that affects other innocent people. Thus, you must coolly and calmly evaluate the situation, the possibilities of a successful apprehension, and then make your decision. If you decide to go for it, you must be able to control both your vehicle and yourself. And you must know when to break off a pursuit when it just plain gets too hairy.

Police officers are drilled in procedure after procedure. As we saw from the Department of Transportation regulations listed previously, officers in a pursuit are given a lot of legal leeway, *if they don't foul up.* Fouling up means getting into an accident, injuring bystanders (or worse), and destroying private property. As we said at the start of this chapter, it's a thankless proposition. If you make a mistake and hurt someone or destroy something, you're suddenly Dirty Harry—an outlaw cop. If you do successfully pursue and apprehend, you're just doing your job.

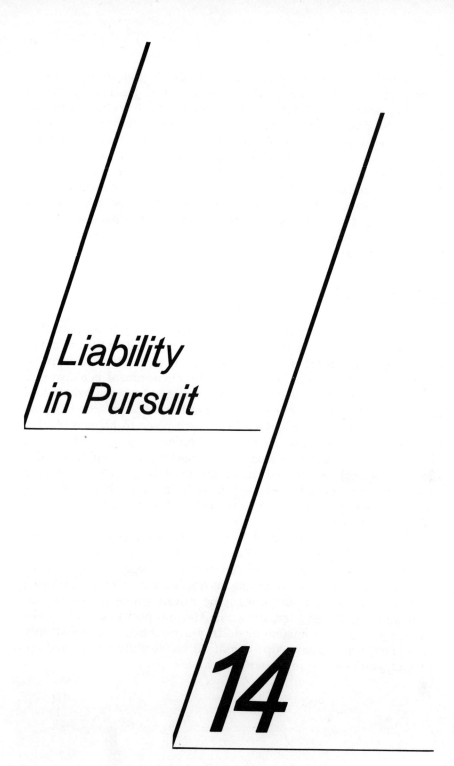

Liability
in Pursuit

14

All states have statutes governing the operation of a motor vehicle. Police officers are no different from any other group of citizens; they have to abide by those laws. Hence, you must understand th. laws regarding the use of your vehicle, just as you must understand your department's guidelines regarding pursuits. Get a copy of the guidelines and read them. Know what you can and cannot do.

There are some general rules of vehicle operation that are basic enough to apply to all law-enforcement officers:

1. The operation of your vehicle is subject to the traffic laws. *All* the traffic laws. Obey all traffic laws unless there is a specific exemption made in state or local statutes. It is for your own benefit that you know these exemptions and follow them to the letter.

2. Whatever the exemptions, you must be in an emergency situation for them to be in effect. Your lights and/or siren must be on (preferably both unless you've been instructed to make a silent approach to the scene of a crime in progress, etc.).

   Case history 1: A police officer was in a cruiser, parked alongside the road. An emergency call came in and the officer pulled out into traffic. While doing so, the officer reached down to turn on the lights and siren. Before the officer could do that, a car came along and hit the cruiser. Although both cars were moving slowly, occupants of the other car, an elderly couple, were killed. When the officer went to court, the decision went against the officer. *Moral:* If you are about to go into an emergency mode, put your lights and siren on first. Do not move the car an inch without knowing that your emergency equipment is on.

3. If you follow local and/or state statutes to the letter and get involved in an accident that results in property damage, loss of life, or injury, you can be held criminally and/or civilly liable. And now for the really bad news. You and your vehicle don't even have to be directly involved in the accident for this to occur. If someone feels you caused the accident, even though your car was not directly involved, you could be held liable.

   Case history 2: A police officer is engaged in a pursuit. The party under pursuit manages to lose the officer and drive up a one-way street—the wrong way. A collision ensues. Multiple deaths result. Although the police officer was not directly involved and was nowhere near the site at the time of the accident, the officer is sued for forcing the party under pursuit to

147

go down a one-way street the wrong way. This case is still in court.

THE WORLD OF POLICE PURSUIT DRIVING

If you are involved in an accident during an emergency situation—such as one of the nightmares described above—and do end up in court, your actions will be judged by two criteria:

1. Was the situation a true emergency?
2. Did you exercise due regard for the safety of others?

Just what is *due regard* for the safety of others? An acceptable definition for due regard is that "a reasonably careful person, performing similar duties and under similar circumstances, would act in the same manner." We'll discuss this concept more fully a little later.

You can reduce the chances of being found guilty of negligence if you follow these guidelines:

Be sure the situation you are about to become involved in is a true emergency. If it is a true emergency, the answers to the following questions will be yes:
- Is there a possibility that this situation could cause death or injury to an individual?
- Is there significant property imperilled?
- Is there anything I can do to lessen the severity of this situation?

Once all these questions have been answered in the affirmative, you are free to act in the due regard of others. Your actions now are governed by basic common sense.

The technical name for the kind of law applicable to situations in which one party has been injured by another party is called *tort law*. In many of the cases we discuss here, that other party inadvertently committing the injury is the police officer.

Who should pay for the injuries that result from a police pursuit? The police officer that started the chase? The criminal? Because part of the purpose of a lawsuit is to establish blame, the attorney for the injured party will spend a lot of time trying to convince a jury that the officer did something wrong. Every action committed during your pursuit will be examined under a kind of legal micro-scope and second-guessed. "Experts" will be introduced in court as the defense attempts to convince the judge and/or jury that you did something terribly wrong.

There is a new breed of ambulance chasers, only these lawyers chase cars, cars that have been involved in high-speed pursuits. This new breed is always on hand to pick up the pieces and hand out the business cards. These lawyers will do their best to make something out of nothing, to point the finger of blame at the police officer or the department (whichever has the insurance carrier with the deepest pockets, that is, the ability to pay big dollars in either an out-of-court settlement or a court judgment).

Case history 3.   A police officer is driving into the parking lot of an apartment complex that had a lot of cars stolen from it. Com-ing toward the officer is a new Lincoln Continental driven by a sus-piciously young kid. The youngster pulls the Lincoln out of the lot and parks on the far side of the street. The officer follows slowly and pulls in behind the Lincoln. The kid peels out at high speed. The of-ficer pauses a moment, then decides to give chase. It's very early in the morning and there's virtually no traffic about. The pursuit takes about two and a half miles. The officer sees the Lincoln disappear over a hill and calls into the station to say that the chase speeds are getting too fast and the officer is breaking off the chase. With no place in which to turn the cruiser around, the officer drives over the crest of the hill to make the turn at the next intersection. After reaching the crest of the hill, the officer sees a bizarre sight. The Lincoln and another car are in pieces, scattered all over the road. The Lincoln's driver is not to be found anywhere. The other car's occupants aren't as lucky. One is dead; the other is severly injured. The officer calls for assistance, then administers first aid to the sur-vivor and more than likely is responsible for saving that person's life. Did our officer receive a commendation for doing a good job? After all, the officer did show good judgment in calling off the pursuit when speeds became excessive and the accident victim's life was saved.

No, our gallant officer was sued for forcing the Lincoln to run the red light that resulted in the Lincoln hitting the other vehicle. This lawsuit was brought even though the officer was far enough away from the scene of the accident at the time of impact that the officer never saw or heard it.

Half-way through the trial there was an out-of-court settlement.

ACCEPTABLE RISK REVISITED

It is obvious that society and the legal system have no idea, no clear view, of just what an acceptable risk is. Despite the obvious fact that the officer in the above case history exercised due care for the public during the pursuit, the officer was sued anyway. And lost.

Accidents resulting in civil suits come in several varieties. The first is the routine traffic suit, the sort of auto accident you can get into while on routine patrol. On routine patrol, you and your cruiser are just like any other motor vehicle and operator, and you should be judged as such. In the real world, however, that's not true. The fact that you are an officer in a cruiser makes you a much more visible target for lawsuits. This means you have to be especially careful.

The second major breed of lawsuit stems from emergency runs. Police officers have driving privileges other drivers do not have, but those privileges are in effect only while you are in emergency mode. If you become involved in an accident under these conditions, you will have to prove you were in this mode for a good legal reason and that your actions did not present an unreasonable risk to the public.

Let's examine a few specific situations. The public is required by law to yield the right-of-way to police vehicles using their lights and sirens. What if a driver, for whatever reason, does not yield the right-of-way? What do you do then? You cannot physically force the motorist out of your way, and you cannot force the motorist to do something that would result in an accident. So what do you do? You have to decide quickly because you are more than likely bearing down on the motorist at a high rate of speed. To be fair, you must give drivers time to react to your lights and siren, time to overcome the initial shock you cause them (because no matter how innocent and law-abiding they really are, they'll always think you're after *them*). You have to give them time to clear their heads and consider what to do to get out of your way.

Most state statutes (review your local laws and know them, please!) allow you to do otherwise illegal things such as drive the wrong way down a one-way street, pass in a no-passing zone, etc., but those laws do not absolve you of the responsibility to exercise due caution. It's usually just a case of plain old common sense.

For example, it's permissible to pass in a no-passing zone as long as you have made sure the road ahead is clear and that there are no intersections ahead. But under no conditions would it ever be a good idea to pass on a hill, or a blind curve. These actions do more than break the law; they more than likely will end your life.

Never try to force a car off the road. There is no way that action can be defended in the event of third-party injury.

If by now you're beginning to feel as if the entire burden of responsibility lies in the hands of the officer behind the wheel, that's good. Because that's the way it is.

Communications

Communications between you and your station during a pursuit are vitally important. Messages should be brief but informative. Always advise the dispatcher what you're doing. Never say anything you wouldn't want a judge to hear. Remember that if an accident occurs, recordings and/or transcripts of your conversations with the dispatcher will probably be introduced in court as part of the public record for everyone to see and hear.

Case history 4. While in pursuit, an officer makes some ethnic remarks about the driver of the car being pursued. The car under pursuit collides with another car. Fatalities result. During the trial, a recording of the communications between the officer and the dispatcher is played for the judge and jury. Of course, the recording contains all of the officer's colorful and oh-so-witty ethnic remarks. Take a wild guess at the ethnic background of not only the presiding judge but also some members of the jury. Now guess who lost the case. Be careful of what you say over the radio and keep your remarks (and prejudices) to yourself.

During the pursuit, keep in regular contact with the dispatcher and provide as much information as possible. If you're alone in the car, be careful about when you decide to communicate with the dispatcher. You don't want to juggle a microphone in one hand while holding the wheel with the other, trying to take a corner at high speed. You'll have to judge just when you can risk taking one hand off the wheel to make a radio call. *This is tricky, so be careful.*

If you have a partner, it's best to have that person handle the radio while you do the driving. No matter if you're alone or with a partner, by far the best time to communicate is when you are driving in a straight line.

When you begin your pursuit, give the dispatcher the following information:

- Suspect vehicle's license plate number.
- Car make and model.

- Number of passengers.
- Description of the violators and whether you have any reason to believe they are armed.
- Anything that can identify the vehicle.
- Your own location.
- The direction you are traveling. If you lose sight of the suspect, inform the dispatcher and give your location at that moment.
- If you decide to call off the pursuit, inform the dispatcher and give your location.

The central problem with pursuit is that the person you're pursuing has obviously done something bad enough that this individual is willing to take the chance of personal injury to oneself and others by driving like an utter lunatic in order to evade apprehension. Without hesitation, you can be assured that the violator will:

- Run people off the road.
- Disregard all traffic signals.
- Try to run you, a police officer, off the road.

As the officer in pursuit, your main concern is the other motorists on the road. They will more than likely get out of the violator's way, then forget to think that someone might really be chasing that individual, someone like you. Other motorists might pull out in front of you. They may see you coming and overreact, perhaps colliding with another car in their haste to get out of the way. The very worst thing they can do is jam on the brakes as you come up from behind them at pursuit speeds.

Felony pursuits are the worst kind by far. The person you are chasing has nothing to lose by running away. Speeding felons are especially bad if they are young kids, because they too have nothing to lose (the court will probably treat them as juveniles, no matter how serious their crime) and their driving skills are not very good. Drunks are bad because they can't even drive at slow speeds safely.

Some pursuits, such as short chases after a traffic-law violator, are not too hazardous, although there is no such thing as a completely safe pursuit. For your sake, pursuit of a traffic-law violator should not become a high-speed race through crowded traffic, because in the event of an accident you're going to have a tough time explaining your rationale to the judge. You may think your answer is a simple and straightforward one ("They broke the law"), but a good lawyer will take apart that response to make you sound like Attila the Hun, chasing this unfortunate citizen, frightening and goading the defendant to drive faster than anyone should, and that the defendant's only violation was in running a stop sign. It may sound ridiculous, but cases like this have happened.

When should a pursuit be called off? For that you have to rely on your own judgment at the time of the pursuit. Use the points listed below as a guide to help you decide when it's just not worth it to continue the chase:

1. When speeds become excessively dangerous.
2. If you suspect your car has a mechanical malfunction, *especially* if you suspect something is wrong with your brakes.
3. When traffic conditions become prohibitively dangerous not just to you but to the general public as well.
4. If the suspect has a car with so much more power than yours that you simply cannot catch up.

You can help yourself before any potential pursuits in your patrol area by mapping the area in your mind long before you ever have to drive it at high speed. Make sure you know where the sharp curves are, along with the blind intersections, playgrounds, schools, blind hills, blind corners, etc. This knowledge tucked away in your head may give you a substantial advantage over your quarry.

GENERAL DRIVING TIPS WHILE IN PURSUIT

1. Keep a safe distance from the suspect. Review Chapter 8 on braking.
2. If you must brake from a high speed, do not jam on the brakes and lock up your wheels. Remember also that it's frequently easier to drive around an object than to stop in front of it. You have a steering wheel as well as brakes to get you out of trouble.
3. If you are running a red light, scan the intersection before you enter it. Remember, speed affects peripheral vision, so the faster you go, the less you can see. Review Chapter 12 on peripheral vision.
4. If you must pass, do it quickly, keeping to a minimum the amount of time spent in the oncoming lane.
5. Don't join a "parade" of police cruisers chasing a suspect unless specifically ordered to do so by a superior.

6. Never block the road with your car unless so ordered.

7. Never pull alongside the violator. Doing so is an open invitation for the violator to force you off the road.

You can help yourself out of court by remembering some basics. If there is an accident as the result of a pursuit, the officer bears the burden of proving that he or she was responding to an emergency. An important point here is that there doesn't have to be an emergency, only that the officer has to *believe* that there is one.

LEGAL RULINGS

The test for determining whether a publicly owned vehicle is responding to an actual emergency or one that merely exists in the mind of the officer in command is a mixed matter of law and fact. Whether the vehicle is being used in an officially designated emergency depends on the nature of the call and the situation as then presented to the mind of the driver. This is why it's so important that you record all communications during an emergency. Introduced as evidence in court, your conversations with the dispatcher could be instrumental in showing how you determined you were in an emergency situation.

Emergency-vehicle statutes impose a duty upon the officers to:

1. Exercise due regard for the safety of others in light of the circumstances of the emergency, or

2. That the officer must not act with reckless disregard for the safety of others.

Due regard for the safety of others is that degree of care which a reasonably prudent man would have used in the discharge of official duties of like nature and like circumstances . . . . While it is desirable that a police officer overtake and apprehend a criminal who he is pursuing, it is equally important that innocent persons, whether or not connected with the emergency to be met, not be maimed or killed in the attempt. (*Archer* v. *Johnson*, Georgia appellate court, 1954)

No matter what the emergency, you must have a working set of lights and siren, as was shown in *Cotten* v. *Transamerica Insurance Co.* (Louisiana appellate court, 1968). In this case, an officer responding to an emergency call ran a red light and collided with the plaintiff. The officer was driving an unmarked car at the time. The headlights were flashing; the siren was also on but emitted only a muffled sound "like a bumblebee" in the words of one witness.

Louisiana exempts emergency vehicles from ordinary traffic regulations as long as they provide an adequate warning to others and exercise due care for the safety of others. In this case, the court found that the "bumblebee" siren was just too feeble and incapable of warning others of the vehicle's approach. Without an adequate siren, the officer was found not exempted from standing traffic regulations. Thus, running the red light was unauthorized and constituted negligence per se.

The lesson to be learned from this is an obvious one. Make sure your lights and siren are in working order before you take on an emergency call. If they aren't working properly and you do go out on call, you're taking an enormous and completely unnecessary risk.

Probably the most tragic type of accident is when an innocent third party is injured, or worse, by the vehicle under pursuit. Most of the time the officer is cleared of any wrongdoing as long as he or she obeyed the guidelines in effect in that jurisdiction. But the officer is still held up to public scrutiny.

In *Roll* v. *Timberman* (N.J., 1967), an officer encountered a parked car with its lights off. As the officer approached, the lights came on and the vehicle shot away at a high rate of speed, failing to halt at a nearby stop sign. The officer gave chase, following for about two miles with both lights and siren on and through a second stop sign without stopping. Chase speeds hit 100 mph. As the fleeing vehicle attempted to pass a truck, it struck the car of a third party, in this case, the plaintiff. The court ruled that the officer was not liable for the results of the criminal's negligence. Police officers cannot be made the insurers of the culprits they chase.

POLICE PURSUIT POLICY

The following are excerpts from the police pursuit policy of the Boston Police Department:*

> It is the position of the Department that law violators be apprehended, whenever apprehension is feasible under the existing conditions. It is not expected, however, that a vehicle be pursued to the point where the life

*All but the paragraph on firearms discharge is from Rule No. 301 of the Boston Police Department, promulgated September, 1974, and rewritten February, 1982. The section on firearms discharge is from Rule 303, Section 9, *Deadly Force*. All excerpts are used with permission from the Boston Police Department.

of the officer, the violator, or others are placed in jeopardy. A high-speed pursuit exposes the officer, the fleeing violator, pedestrians and drivers and passengers of other motor vehicles to the possibility of death or serious injury. Pursuits may also result in damage to personal property.

Definitions.   For the purposes of this rule, the following definitions will apply:

Motorized pursuit is an active attempt to stop a moving motor vehicle when the driver of such vehicle is resisting apprehension by maintaining and increasing . . . speed or by ignoring the officer's attempt to stop him/her.

High-speed pursuit refers to motorized pursuit at speeds that exceed the actual speed limit.

Police vehicle means and includes any Department-owned motor vehicle, in authorized use, or any vehicle authorized by the Police Commissioner for use by a member of the Police Department acting in his or her capacity as a police officer.

General considerations.   Chapter 89, Section 7-B, of the Massachusetts General Laws, *Operations of Emergency Vehicles*, states that:

> The driver of a vehicle of a fire, police or recognized protective department, and the driver of an ambulance shall be subject to the provisions of any statute, rule, regulation, ordinance, or by-law relating to the operation or parking of vehicles, except that drivers of fire apparatus while going to a fire or responding to an alarm, or the driver of a vehicle of a police or recognized protective department or the driver of an ambulance, in an emergency and while in performance of a public duty or while transporting a sick or injured person to a hospital or other destination where professional medical services are available, may drive such vehicle at a speed in excess of the applicable speed limit if [the driver] exercises caution and due regard under the circumstances for the safety of persons and property, and may drive such vehicle through an intersection of ways contrary to any traffic signs or signals regulating full stop and then proceed with caution and due regard for the safety of persons and property unless otherwise directed by a police officer regulating traffic at such intersections.

Before initiating "high-speed" pursuit, officers should attempt to narrow the distance between their vehicle and the violator before turning on the blue lights and siren of their vehicle so that the driver they want to stop may not be alerted prematurely. When a pursuit is undertaken, officers should be prepared to discontinue the pursuit if circumstances indicate that it would be unreasonable to continue.

Officers engaged in high-speed pursuit must weigh the seriousness of the violator's suspected crime against the potential for death, injury, or damage if the pursuit is continued.

Control and coordination.   In all motorized pursuits, the dispatcher has the primary responsibility for coordinating the efforts of all units involved and has the authority to direct that a pursuit be abandoned, or that a high-speed pursuit be limited to two Department vehicles.

Units in the vicinity of a high-speed pursuit shall make their location and availability known to the dispatcher and then follow the dispatcher's instructions.

Abandonment of pursuit.   Department members shall discontinue a high-speed pursuit when ordered to do so by a dispatcher, a Superior Officer, or when traffic and/or weather conditions make further pursuit inordinately dangerous to the officers or the public.

Pursuit with passengers prohibited.   Officers shall not engage in a high-speed pursuit when their vehicle is occupied by prisoners, suspects, complainants, witnesses, or any other persons not on duty as police officers for the City of Boston. This regulation applies whether or not the passenger has signed a waiver of liability.

Use of siren and blue lights.   Officers must conform to the provisions of Massachusetts General Law, Chapter 89, Section 7–B, and use the blue emergency lights and siren of their vehicle when engaged in a high-speed pursuit.

Unmarked units.   Department vehicles which are not equipped with blue lights and a siren *shall not be used in a high-speed pursuit.* Officers assigned to such a vehicle shall notify the dispatcher of the vehicle with which they are concerned, and after providing all information relevant to the vehicle, shall continue to pursue only if they are able to do so at legal speeds.

Transmitting information.   When an officer has started a high-speed pursuit and the pursued operator fails to stop when blue lights and siren are used, the pursuing officer shall immediately inform the dispatcher and transmit the following information:

- The best possible description of the vehicle and its occupants.
- The reason for the pursuit, especially the alleged crime involved.
- The direction of travel and the roadways being used.

Upon receipt of a transmission from a unit engaged in a high-speed pursuit, the dispatcher shall order the frequency cleared, shall deploy additional units as [the dispatcher] deems necessary and shall notify [the] Supervisor.

It is essential that police officers involved in motorized pursuits maintain constant and coherent communication with the police dispatcher.

Operations supervisor. The Operations Supervisor, upon being made aware of the initiation of a high-speed pursuit, by the dispatcher, shall familiarize himself [herself] with the details as soon as it is practicable. [The supervisor] shall monitor the progress of units engaged in the pursuit and shall be prepared to terminate a pursuit when conditions warrant that it should be stopped.

Contact between vehicles. Officers shall avoid deliberate contact with pursued vehicles.

Motorcycle units. If pursuit is initiated by a two-wheel motorcycle unit, the motorcycle unit shall abandon the pursuit when a marked police department four-wheel vehicle is in a position to assume the pursuit.

Firearm discharges. Firearms shall not be discharged at or from a moving vehicle unless the officer is being threatened with deadly force by an occupant of the target vehicle. Under such circumstances, officers should be aware of the usual inability of revolver fire to penetrate the metal or glass surfaces of an automobile. Revolver fire cannot be depended on to stop a moving vehicle. (Rule 303, Section 9, *Deadly Force*)

Pursuit into other jurisdictions. When a pursued vehicle leaves the City of Boston, the pursuing officer shall notify the dispatcher who shall transmit the information outlined in Section 8 to the police department having jurisdiction.

Pursuits by other law enforcement agencies. Unless specifically authorized by a Boston Police Department dispatcher, no unit shall join in a high-speed pursuit initiated by another law enforcement agency. This does not preclude a unit from being assigned to a point of advantage or being dispatched to the scene of a termination of a pursuit to assist officers of another law enforcement agency.

Barricading roadways. Barricading a roadway as a means of stopping a motor vehicle must be considered as likely to result in death or serious injury. Therefore, this method of attempting to stop a pursuit is not used in misdemeanor pursuits, and only as a last resort in felony cases, where the violator constitutes an immediate and continuing threat to the public and all other efforts have failed to stop the subject.

Report of a high-speed pursuit. An officer who participates in a high-speed pursuit shall, before ending his [her] tour of duty, submit a High Speed Pursuit Report Card through appropriate channels, to the superintendent, Bureau of Field Services, in which [the officer] shall detail the reasons for and circumstances of the pursuit.

Supervisor's responsibilities.   If a Supervisor has not responded to a high-speed pursuit, the Operations Division shall dispatch a Supervisor from the District or Unit to which the officers who initiated the pursuit are assigned.

The supervisor shall be responsible for controlling police action at the scene of the termination of a pursuit and ensuring adherence to Department policies. The Supervisor shall retain this responsibility until the termination scene is cleared and all reports completed. The supervisor shall ensure that Form 1647 required by Section 16 of this rule has been submitted.

Police
Vehicles

15

In the good old days, police cruisers were what the hot-rod crowd used to call "sleepers." On the outside, they were boring "gutless wonders," family cars designed to haul kids, spouse, dog, and tons of luggage on the annual family vacation. But underneath their non-descript exteriors beat the heart of a road demon. What would have been considered exotic options on a Detroit assembly-line car was standard equipment on police cruisers: sports car items such as high-compression engines, high-lift cams, multiple carburetors, high numerical rear-axle gear ratios, and suspension systems straight from the great road-racing tracks of Europe. These cars hit top speeds of 150 mph, and their acceleration made the trip from a standstill to 120 mph seem like an afterburner takeoff in an F-16.

These cars were designed and built to be the fastest cars on the road. And there really weren't that many cars that were faster. Today, those hot cars and the economic and social conditions that created them are long gone. Contemporary police cruisers are built to meet all federal safety and emission standards. But because a lot of other cars don't meet these standards, a lot of cars on the road today can easily outrun a police cruiser.

Just what kind of performance can you expect from the contemporary police cruiser? Every year the Michigan State Police conduct tests on Detroit's last batch of cruisers. But before a car can even compete in the competition, it must meet certain minimum requirements. Here's a brief outline of the very minimum a good cruiser should be:

1. Acceleration

    0–60 mph . . . . 13.5 sec or less

    0–80 mph . . . . 24.0 sec or less

    0–100 mph . . . . 45.0 sec or less

Each vehicle must make four acceleration runs. The times are then averaged.

2. A speed of 110 mph must be attained within a 3 mi distance.

    (a) Test vehicles must make four consecutive stops from 90 mph with a constant deceleration rate of 22 ft/sec/sec maintained all the way from 90 mph to zero mph. Immediately after this brake heating procedure, any controlled stop must be made from 60 mph.

    (b) After a four-minute cooling off period, the above test is repeated. Immediately after, with the brakes still heated, each vehicle must complete a panic stop with every wheel locked, from 60 mph. The purpose of these tests is to seek evidence of brake fade and evaluate the vehicle's ability to stop in a straight line staying within a standard highway lane.

Police cruisers must be dependable because, unlike ordinary cars, they aren't driven for brief trips to work or to take the kids to school. They spend dozens of hours on the road at a stretch, in all kinds of weather, on all kinds of road surfaces. After idling by the side of the road for an hour, they have to be ready and able to blast off on pursuit at the press of a pedal. It has to have the handling qualities of a sports car, yet be large enough to squeeze in large officers and unruly prisoners. A police cruiser is a unique automobile.

The heart of any car is the powerplant. Today's cruiser can contain anything from a 135-cu in to a 351-cu in engine. Cruiser engines are exposed to conditions that can literally tear an engine apart. Because the vehicle is often operated at low speeds, left idling, or cruising slowly for long periods of time, carbon deposits build up inside the powerplant, which cause it to lose power. These deposits can be especially troublesome when the engine is suddenly awakened from its automotive hibernation and called to life in a chase down some dark highway.

In comparing a police cruiser with the family car, the casual observer would notice no real external differences between the two vehicles, other than the obvious fact that one has police insignia on the doors and special lights on the roof. The real difference is inside the cars, not outside. Let's take a look at the cruiser's various systems and see just what makes them special:

Air conditioner.   On a cruiser, this is a factory-installed, heavy-duty system designed to prevent component damage from both high-speed driving and long periods of use. Air conditioners are a must for police vehicles, which are generally operated all day long. Cruiser air conditioners must be able to take prolonged use.

Alternator system.   The alternator system consists of a transistorized regulator, 80 amp minimum output capacity, minimum curb idle output of 45 amps at manufacturer's recommended idle speed. A heavy-duty alternator is needed to power the many accessories carried by a cruiser, especially the radio. The family car has no need for this beefy electrical system.

Battery.   It must be a 12-volt battery with 465 cold cranking amps at the very least. Again, a big battery is needed to help power a big electrical system.

Cooling system   The cruiser will have the biggest cooling system that can possibly be installed on this particular design. The system will incorporate a "coolant recovery" system, which is installed at the factory.

Engine.   Cubic-inch displacement is at the manufacturer's option, as long as the car can meet or exceed the performance specifications of the Michigan State Police tests.

Gauges.   An extensive instrument cluster should be standard on any cruiser, including an ammeter or voltmeter, water temperature and oil pressure gauges, preferably located in the instrument cluster, or under the dash convenient to the driver. Instruments are an absolute must. "Idiot lights" (as indicator lights are sometimes called) aren't very helpful for police work. If you are in a pursuit and your oil pressure light comes on, the only thing you're really being told is that the engine is going to blow up in about five seconds if you don't turn it off immediately. This sort of information is neither timely nor helpful.

Glass.   All windows should be the heat-absorbing tinted type.

Headlights.   Quartz-halogen high-beam headlights should be standard. These are amazing lights that permit superior long-distance vision.

BASIC COMPONENT SPECIFICATIONS

Transmission.   This should be at least a three-speed transmission, fully automatic, and the heaviest-duty model available. The transmission should include an automatic override to prevent it from being accidentally downshifted into low gear. Downshifting an automatic transmission into low gear at high speeds will generally destroy the transmission.

Rear axle.   Like the rest of the cruiser's drivetrain, this should be a heavy-duty component. The desired gear ratios can usually be ordered. The ratio offered by the factory as first choice will be compatible with the performance and economy requirements of that particular design. A limited amount of slip in the differential is a must.

Suspension. Again, heavy-duty suspension, including shock absorbers, front and rear, is mandatory. In addition, front and rear heavy-duty stabilizer bars provide the best combination of suspension qualities to reduce body roll and provide flat cornering. Stabilizer bars should not extend below the lowest point on the vehicle chassis.

Brakes. Power disc brakes for the front wheels, drums or discs for the rear, are recommended. Brakes should have heavy-duty semi-metallic or fully metallic-type linings or their wet and dry equivalent.

Steering. With police cars getting smaller and officers getting bigger, power steering with a power steering cooler is the best way to go. Tilted steering wheels are a must for comfort.

Wheelbase. This can change on a yearly basis. Current requirement: 118 in maximum, 108.9 in minimum.

Electrical. A maintenance-free battery of no less than a 70 amp/hour rating is required. Alternator output should be no less than 61 amps, and at least 35 amps at 700 engine rpm. The dual belt drive system is preferable. All belts, whether dual or single, should be high-performance quality. Windshield wipers should have two speeds. Each car should have a single-key locking system, including the locks for trunk and glove compartment. All cruisers in the department fleet should be keyed alike and each car should have four keys.
The engine compartment hood should have a release latch located slightly under the dash at the driver's side. The control for the hood release should feel sufficiently different from that of the emergency brake so that there is no chance of confusing the two.

Mirrors. Outside rearview mirrors should be made of nonglare glass and mounted on the doors left and right. Minimum mirror area is 14 square inches.

VEHICLE SIZE

Like it or not, in the future we will all drive small cars. Most of us do already. The shrinking American car is causing a reevaluation of just what a small car is. What we would have considered a small car 20 years ago is a good-sized sedan today. Yet, as cars shrink, they manage to retain a good deal of room on the inside. Car doors and walls are thinner; powerplants smaller. So just what is small and what is large? Thanks to the federal Environmental Protection Agency (EPA), we no longer have to argue about car sizes. The EPA ranks cars by both interior dimensions and luggage capacity into four groups.

1. *Subcompact*—Vehicles with less than 100 cu ft of passenger and luggage volume, and a wheelbase* of just under 100 in.
2. *Compact*—Vehicles with 100 to 110 cu ft of passenger and luggage space with wheelbases from 100 to 106 in.
3. *Intermediate*—Vehicles with 110 to 120 cu ft of passenger and luggage space with wheelbases from 106 to 114 in.
4. *Full size*—More than 120 cu ft of passenger and luggage space with wheelbases of 114 in and up.

Small cars use less fuel. But a closer look at EPA fuel consumption figures for small cars indicates that fleets of small cars don't necessarily mean lower overall levels of fuel consumption.

Most manufacturers' fuel consumption claims show the fuel specifics for the most stripped-down version of that particular model, using a four- or five-speed transmission. As we know, police vehicles use heavy-duty equipment, and this equipment, transported by a drivetrain featuring an automatic transmission, cuts the gas mileage of any make or model car significantly. The EPA mileage figures, treated as Gospel truth by the carmakers, are extremely unrealistic figures, but the fault really isn't the EPA's. Most of us assume that gas mileage figures are obtained through extensive road testing. This is simply not true. Instead, the car is attached to a sort of huge indoor treadmill, known as a *dynamometer.* This is done in order to subject each car to a uniform test, with all cars treated alike. But to anyone who has ever jogged on both a treadmill and out on the open road, the difference is obvious. There are no hills on treadmills, no stop-and-go traffic, no bad weather, no bumpy roads. It is a very unrealistic running experience, and likewise, a very unrealistic driving experience.

What the EPA test figures are good for is a reliable comparison between makes and models of various cars, for they all receive the same tests.

*The wheelbase is the distance from the center line of the front tire to the center line of the rear tire.

Therefore, consider the EPA figures of a particular vehicle equipped as it will be purchased. You may discover that the savings just aren't that good. The fuel-efficient cars that fill the transportation needs of the department will be a compromise between economy and performance—a happy medium depending on the car's *driveline*—the combination of engine, transmission, and differential.

The smallest engine is *not* always the most fuel-efficient. Some of the larger cars originally designed for big, beefy V-8 power offer an "economy six" option that makes very little difference in mpg. Moreover, the economy six is less powerful and wears out more rapidly.

In the same way, cars designed for six-cylinder engines are now available with four cylinders. To be realistic, a small engine in an option-loaded car simply will not have the pulling power needed by a police vehicle. Overworking the smaller engine will lead to a higher breakdown rate and higher maintenance costs, which offset the potential fuel savings. In some cases, the larger engine is the superior choice for overall economy.

A final point: An automobile is not a passive conveyance. It's connected to an alive and active driver. You, behind the wheel, with your feet on the pedals, are one of the most important factors in the fuel efficiency of your automobile.

FUEL ECONOMY

Recently the Department of Transportation issued a report on the impact of fuel costs on law enforcement. It found that fuel costs are the second-largest budget item, after salaries, for the vast majority of police departments, whether they be state, county, or municipal.

Much can be accomplished to offset increased fuel costs through carefully tailored but relatively minor changes in force deployment, equipment choices, maintenance procedures, and other conservation-related activities. What follows are a few ideas, comments, and remedies.

Maximized Fuel Cost

Pay close attention to the lubrication, oil, and fuel requirements of your vehicle fleet. Neglect these three critical areas and you run the risk of major damage to motor and mechanical parts, resulting in extensive vehicle downtime.

Check regularly for oil and lubrication needs. Consider the new generation of synthetic oils. They can offer faster starts, less maintenance, faster heat dissipation, and longer engine life, especially in regions of the country that experience weather extremes. By using synthetic oil, a fuel savings of about 2.5 percent can be expected because of lowered friction. Admittedly, synthetics are expensive but can pay off in the long run.

Dirty oil cuts fuel economy and engine life. Change your oil and oil filter at the manufacturer's specified mileages.

Keep your gas tanks at least half full. By keeping the bottom half of the tank full, you reduce the likelihood of water condensation in the fuel system and fuel contamination overall, along with fuel waste and maintenance downtime.

Fuel octane rates are going down. This can decrease engine life and performance and damage the powerplant through deterioration (premature firing of the fuel/air mixture in the cylinder). An improperly adjusted or malfunctioning carburetor can waste up to three mpg. A misfiring spark plug can waste another two mpg. Another mile of gas mileage can be tossed away because of a dirty air filter. Loose or worn fan and compressor belts waste engine power. Dragging brake pucks can steal mileage through excessive drag. All these combined add up to a loss of six mpg. But they can be cured with a tune-up. Properly tuned police cruisers, like any car, run better, get better gas mileage, and can supply you with the extra horsepower you need when you need it. Have maintenance check these items regularly.

Tire Inflation

Improperly inflated tires can mean a loss of between one and four mpg. Check tire pressure regularly, even daily. Tires get a lot of use. A 35-degree increase in air temperature can lower tire pressures three to five pounds. Low pressure leads to tire failures, which means downtime, or accidents.

And while you're checking your tires, don't forget the one tire everyone forgets until it's too late—the spare.

Make daily visual inspection of your tires with pressure gauge in hand. Use it and take tire pressure, just as a doctor routinely takes a patient's temperature.

Keep snow tires on the cruiser only as long as needed. They're designed for use on snow and aren't very good on other surfaces. Regular tread tires provide the best mileage and keep noise and vibration levels low.

Other Fuel-Saving Tips

Check all vehicle fluid levels daily. Low levels of coolant, power-steering fluid, transmission fluid, oil, and differential fluids can lead to increased fuel consumption through increased friction, and this friction can, in turn, bring on early failures.

Roof light bars and other externally mounted equipment should be selected and installed to be as aerodynamically efficient as possible. Secure them tightly to reduce noise levels and vibration, not to mention possible loss if they are *really* loose.

Long idling to maintain a comfortable internal car temperature in winter results in higher fuel consumption. If you live in cool climates consider equipping your vehicles with devices such as "auto therm," which circulates engine coolant through the heater when the engine is off.

The average patrol vehicle spends approximately one hour per shift with the motor running unnecessarily at idle. This practice can consume one to three mpg per shift and can cause harmful engine deposit buildups. Gas consumed in a minute of idling can propell the vehicle for four miles of patrol.

A cruiser requires less gas to restart than it takes to idle for 15 seconds. Shut off your engine whenever possible.

Radar-checking teams should turn off engines during periods of intermittent activity. Cars operating radar should idle to maintain electrical output. Shut off the engine while writing citations—even when investigating an accident after power needs for illumination are no longer needed. Issue engine operating instructions to radar and accident investigation teams.

Jackrabbit Starts

Here's an example of how we can conserve gasoline simply by driving conservatively:

FUEL USED

- Maximum acceleration: 8.5 mpg (jackrabbit start)
- Accelerate with traffic: 12.5 mpg (normal start)
- Mild acceleration: 14.7 mpg (easy start)

Maximum acceleration causes transmission and engine strains that lead to major repairs.

Trunk Contents

Every extra 100 pounds of weight carried costs about 1/2 mpg and cuts down performance. Remember that heavy police equipment that was easily carried in the trunks of older, bigger cars may result in handling problems, even headlight alignment problems, in today's smaller, lighter cars.

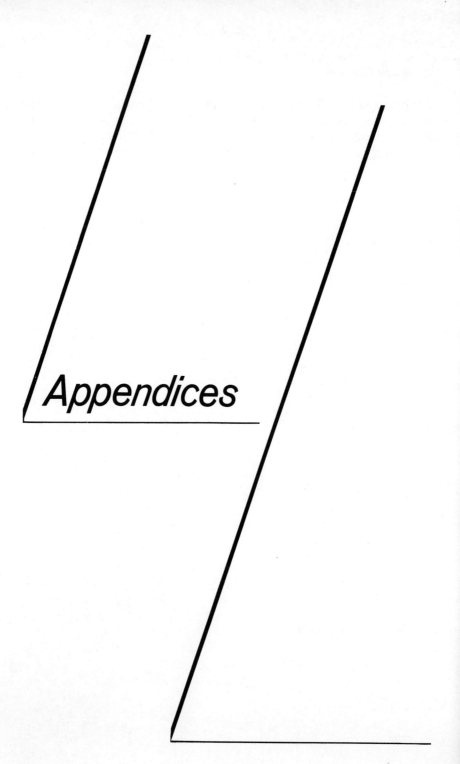

Appendices

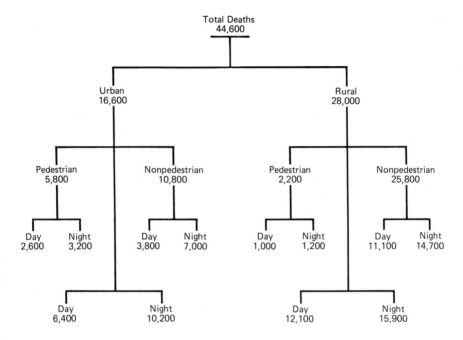

Figure A-1 Gross breakdown of U.S. annual highway fatalities—when, where, and to whom they occur. Reprinted courtesy of National Safety Council.

APPENDIX B

DIRECTION MOTOR VEHICLES WERE TRAVELING
WHEN INVOLVED IN ACCIDENTS, 1981-83

	Fatal Accidents			All Accidents		
	Total	Urban	Rural	Total	Urban	Rural
Pedestrian						
Intersection	2.9	6.8	0.9	0.1	0.2	0.1
Nonintersection	15.6	27.6	8.1	0.4	0.4	0.3
Nontraffic	1.0	2.3	0.3			
Two Motor Vehicles						
Intersection	14.5	16.9	12.5	44.9	51.4	28.6
Nonintersection	24.7	15.6	30.7	34.8	35.6	32.2
Nontraffic	0.3	0.2	0.3			
All Other Collisions						
Intersections	0.9	1.7	0.6	1.1	1.4	0.6
Nonintersection	10.0	11.9	8.7	4.2	4.0	4.5

Note: All statistics are in percent.
Reprinted courtesy of National Safety Council.

APPENDIX C

FORCE ACTING ON THE CAR *VS.* CORNER RADIUS AND SPEED

Speed (mph)	50	60	70	80	90	100
	G-Forces Acting on the Car					
10	0.134	0.112	0.096	0.084	0.075	0.067
12	0.193	0.161	0.138	0.121	0.107	0.097
14	0.263	0.219	0.188	0.164	0.146	0.132
16	0.344	0.286	0.245	0.215	0.191	0.172
18	0.435	0.362	0.311	0.272	0.242	0.217
20	0.537	0.447	0.383	0.336	0.298	0.268
22	0.650	0.541	0.464	0.406	0.361	0.325
24	0.773	0.644	0.552	0.483	0.429	0.387
26	0.907	0.756	0.648	0.567	0.504	0.454
28	1.05	0.877	0.752	0.658	0.585	0.526
30	1.21	1.01	0.863	0.755	0.671	0.604
32	1.37	1.15	0.982	0.859	0.764	0.687
34	1.55	1.29	1.11	0.970	0.862	0.776
36	1.74	1.45	1.24	1.09	0.966	0.870
38	1.94	1.62	1.38	1.21	1.08	0.969
40	2.15	1.79	1.53	1.34	1.19	1.07

APPENDIX D

REACTION TIME VS. DISTANCE TRAVELED

Distance Traveled (in Seconds)

Reaction Time (in Seconds)

Speed mph	0.1	0.2	0.3	0.4	0.5	0.6	0.7	0.8	0.9	1.0
10	1.47	2.94	4.41	5.88	7.35	8.82	10.29	11.76	13.23	14.7
12	1.764	3.528	5.292	7.056	8.82	10.58	12.35	14.11	15.88	17.64
14	2.058	4.116	6.174	8.232	10.29	12.35	14.41	16.46	18.52	20.58
16	2.352	4.704	7.056	9.408	11.76	14.11	16.46	18.82	21.17	23.52
18	2.646	5.292	7.938	10.58	13.23	15.88	18.52	21.17	23.81	26.46
20	2.94	5.88	8.82	11.76	14.7	17.64	20.58	23.52	26.46	29.4
22	3.234	6.468	9.702	12.94	16.17	19.40	22.64	25.87	29.11	32.34
24	3.528	7.056	10.58	14.11	17.64	21.17	24.70	28.22	31.75	35.28
26	3.822	7.644	11.47	15.29	19.11	22.93	26.75	30.58	34.40	38.22
28	4.116	8.232	12.35	16.46	20.58	24.70	28.81	32.93	37.04	41.16
30	4.41	8.82	13.23	17.64	22.05	26.46	30.87	35.28	39.69	44.1
32	4.704	9.408	14.11	18.82	23.52	28.22	32.93	37.63	42.34	47.04
34	4.998	9.996	14.99	19.99	24.99	29.99	34.99	39.98	44.98	49.98
36	5.292	10.58	15.88	21.17	26.46	31.75	37.04	42.34	47.63	52.92
38	5.586	11.17	16.76	22.34	27.93	33.52	39.10	44.69	50.27	55.86

Distance Traveled (in Seconds)

5.88	11.76	17.64	23.52	29.4	35.28	41.16	47.04	52.92	58.8	40
6.174	12.35	18.52	24.70	30.87	37.04	43.22	49.39	55.57	61.74	42
6.468	12.94	19.40	25.87	32.34	38.81	45.28	51.74	58.21	64.68	44
6.762	13.52	20.29	27.05	33.81	40.57	47.33	54.10	60.86	67.62	46
7.056	14.11	21.17	28.22	35.28	42.34	49.39	56.45	63.50	70.56	48
7.35	14.7	22.05	29.4	36.75	44.1	51.45	58.8	66.15	73.5	50
7.644	15.29	22.93	30.58	38.22	45.86	53.51	61.15	68.80	76.44	52
7.938	15.88	23.81	31.75	39.69	47.63	55.57	63.50	71.44	79.38	54
8.232	16.46	24.70	32.93	41.16	49.39	57.62	65.86	74.09	82.32	56
8.526	17.05	25.58	34.10	42.63	51.16	59.68	68.21	76.73	85.26	58
8.82	17.64	26.46	35.28	44.1	52.92	61.74	70.56	79.38	88.2	60
9.114	18.23	27.34	36.46	45.57	54.68	63.80	72.91	82.03	91.14	62
9.408	18.82	28.22	37.63	47.04	56.45	65.86	75.26	84.67	94.08	64
9.702	19.40	29.11	38.81	48.51	58.21	67.91	77.62	87.32	97.02	66
9.996	19.99	29.99	39.98	49.98	59.98	69.97	79.97	89.96	99.96	68
10.29	20.58	30.87	41.16	51.45	61.74	72.03	82.32	92.61	102.9	70
10.58	21.17	31.75	42.34	52.92	63.50	74.09	84.67	95.26	105.8	72
10.88	21.76	32.63	43.51	54.39	65.27	76.15	87.02	97.90	108.8	74
11.17	22.34	33.52	44.69	55.86	67.03	78.20	89.38	100.5	111.7	76
11.47	22.93	34.40	45.86	57.33	68.80	80.26	91.73	103.2	114.7	78
11.76	23.52	35.28	47.04	58.8	70.56	82.32	94.08	105.8	117.6	80

APPENDIX E

CONVERSION OF MPH TO FPS

mph	fps
10	14.7
12	17.64
14	20.58
16	23.52
18	26.46
20	29.4
22	32.34
24	35.28
26	38.22
28	41.16
30	44.1
32	47.04
34	49.98
36	52.92
38	55.86
40	58.8
42	61.74
44	64.68
46	67.62
48	70.56
50	73.5
52	76.44
54	79.38
56	82.32
58	85.26
60	88.2
62	91.14
64	94.08
66	97.02
68	99.96
70	102.9
72	105.84
74	108.78
76	111.72
78	114.66
80	117.6

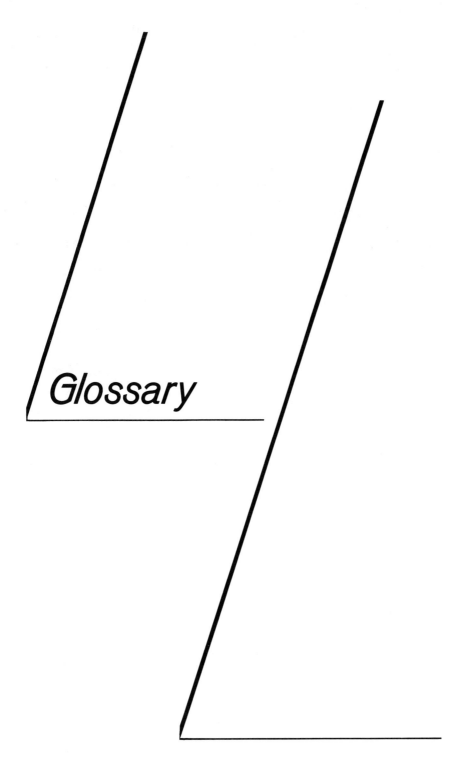

Glossary

Acceleration The rate of which the velocity of a vehicle increases per unit of time.

Apex The imaginary point in a corner where the tire touches the inside of the road.

Body Lean The tendency for the body of the car to lean as the driver turns the steering wheel.

Brake Fade A problem brought about by heavy use of the brakes. Usually occurs during a pursuit when the officer presses on the brake but the vehicle does not slow down.

Centrifugal Force The force exerted on the car when the driver moves the steering wheel. Also called *cornering power.* If too much force is applied, the car can lose control.

Coefficient of Friction The ratio of the friction between the tire and the road. It's this friction that keeps the car attached to the road. The greater the coefficient of friction the more the vehicle will stick to the road.

Constant Radius Corner A corner where the radius stays the same as you drive through. This type corner would end in a circle.

Cornering The ability of the vehicle to track the path determined by the front tires. The path of the front tires is determined by the driver.

Deceleration The rate of change of speed as the vehicle slows down.

Decreasing Radius Corner The corner gets sharper as you drive around it. An example would be an off-ramp on a highway.

Emergency Mode Driving to an emergency with the lights and siren on.

Fear Factor God's way of telling us that whatever we are doing we ought not to be doing.

Feet per Second A more practical way of explaining speed. Can be determined by multiplying miles per hour by 1.47.

Front Wheel Skid The front wheels have lost their adhesion to the ground and the vehicle does not travel in the direction that it is being steered.

G's A method of explaining the amount of force being applied to the vehicle. One G would be the weight of the car.

Hydroplaning When the grooves on the tires fill to the point that the tires do not make contact with the road. The result is loss of control.

Increasing Radius Corner The exit of the corner becomes less sharp.

Kinetic Energy The energy that a car builds up because of its speed. This is a very important aspect of driving, because it is this energy that the driver must control when operating the vehicle.

Lateral Acceleration The force pushing on the side of the car moving it away from the inside of the corner. The important thing is that the force is not linear. If you double the speed you increase the lateral acceleration by a factor of four.

Limit of Adhesion The maximum performance available from a vehicle. It is determined by the adhesion of the car to the road.

Locked Wheels When the wheels stop turning and the tires start to slide. A very dangerous condition because if the front wheels are locked (stop turning) the driver has also lost steering control.

Momentum A vehicle in motion wants to stay in motion, until it is overcome by another force.

Oversteer A term used to describe the handling characteristics of a car. Means that the back of the car is breaking away from the driver.

Reaction Time The time it takes for the brain to receive information from the senses, make a decision, transmit the decision to the appropriate muscles, and the time for the muscles to respond.

Rear Wheel Skid The rear wheels have lost their grip with the road, causing the back of the car to swing out.

Ride The vertical motion of the tires moving up and down according to the road's irregularities. A good-riding car isolates the driver from the road.

Rolling Friction Term used to describe the friction created by the tires as they are rolling over the ground.

Tire Contact Patch The area of the tire that makes contact with the ground. All the control of the vehicle is done through these tire patches.

Weight Transfer The movement of the vehicle's weight fore and aft or side to side. Caused because of acceleration, braking, or turning of the steering wheel.

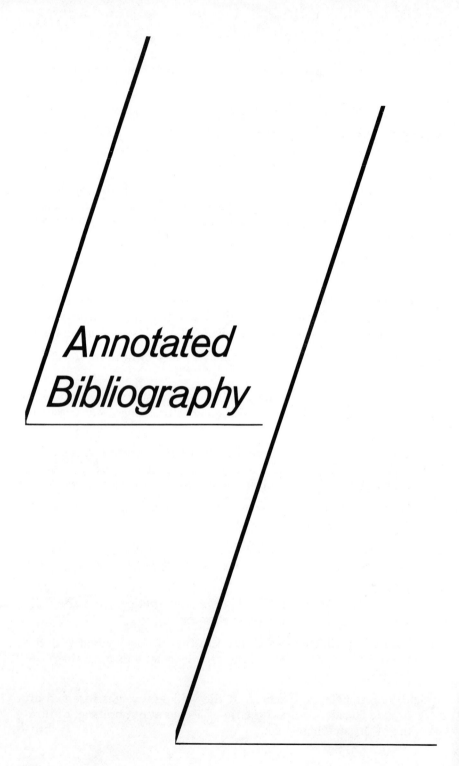

Annotated Bibliography

ACCIDENT CAUSATION. A collection of papers that discuss why we get into accidents. Produced by the Society of Automotive Engineers.

BLINCOE, LAWRENCE J., AND LUCHTER, STEPHEN. "The Economic Cost to Society of Motor Vehicle Accidents." Society of Automotive Engineers Technical Series No. 830614. Society of Automotive Engineers, 400 Commonwealth Drive, Warrendale, Pa. 15096.

BREWER, HOWELL K., AND RICE, ROY S. "Tires, Stability and Control." Society of Automotive Engineers Paper 830561. Explanation of how tires affect vehicle control.

CAR AND DRIVER. A magazine that is "must" reading for anyone involved in driving professionally.

GILLIS, JACK. *The Car Book.* New York: Harper & Row. A comprehensive outline on cars and driving with no attachments to the auto industry.

GOODYEAR TIRE AND RUBBER COMPANY. "Radial Auto Tire Service Manual." Akron, Ohio 44316.

MAEDA, TERUO. "Performance of Driver-Vehicle System in Emergency Avoidance." Society of Automotive Engineers Paper 770130. An analysis of how drivers perform in an emergency situation.

MOSKOWITZ, HERBERT. "Alcohol and Drug Impairment of the Driver." Society of Automotive Engineers Paper 730094.

NATIONAL SAFETY COUNCIL. "Accident Facts." 444 N. Michigan Ave., Chicago, Ill. 60611. Good source for up-to-date data on accident rates.

SHADLE, SCOTT G., AND EMERY, LLOYD H. "Vehicle Braking Stability and Control." Society of Automotive Engineers Paper 830567. Explanation of how the lighting system in a car is affected by the elements.

TARUFFI, PIERO. "The Technique of Motor Racing." Robert Bentley Publishing, 872 Massachusetts Ave., Cambridge, Mass. 02139. A very old book, but still the best explanation of how to drive a car around a corner.

TRANSPORTATION RESEARCH BOARD. "Highway Safety Literature." 2101 Constitution Ave., N.W., Washington, D.C. 20418. A guide of where to go to get information on highway safety. Published quarterly and is an excellent guide to finding information about anything to do with automotive safety.

U.S. DEPARTMENT OF TRANSPORTATION, NATIONAL HIGHWAY TRAFFIC SAFETY ADMINISTRATION. "Training Program for Operation of Emergency Vehicles." A comprehensive manual on how to conduct driver-training programs. Can be ordered from the U.S. Government Printing Office.

WATERGATE 600. "Insurance Institute for Highway Safety." Washington, D.C. 20037. A twice-a-month publication filled with automotive safety news. The organization is nonprofit, and has no axe to grind with the automotive industry.

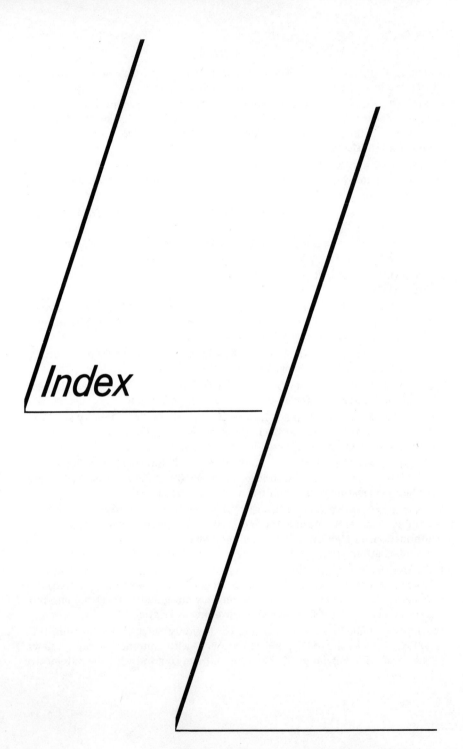

Index

Right-side mirror, 92
Risk taking:
  acceptable, in pursuit, 150-51
  due to fatigue, 13
Road barricades, 158
Road conditions:
  corners and curves, 74-79
  and driving system, 20
  exaggeration of flaws at high speeds,
    130-31
  and limit of adhesion, 53
  weather-related, 79-82
  (see also Dry roads; Icy roads;
    Snowy roads; Wet roads)
Rods, of eye, 117, 118
Roll bars, 114
Rolling friction, 49, 179
Roll v. Timberman, 155
Roof light bars, 168

Saab 900 Turbo, G-force rating, 60
Safe area, for turning, 38
Safe driving, foundation of, 10-11
Seat belts, 16-17
  how to wear, 17
  to reduce fatigue, 14
Seating position, 14, 105
Serengeti Drivers, 120
Shock absorbers, 55
Shoulder harnasses, 114
Side collisions, 22
Sideview mirrors, 11, 92
Signaling:
  before passing, 34
  for turn at intersection, 37
  for two-point turns, 40
  for U-turn, 38
Single-car accidents, 23
Siren:
  limitation of, 143-45, 155
  use before backing up, 43
  (see also Emergency mode; Lights
    and siren)
Skids, 67-68
  four-wheel, 67-68
  front-wheel, 68, 178
  due to improper braking, 84, 87
  rear-wheel, 68, 179
Skills, for high-speed driving, 126-27

Slalom exercises, 105, 107
Slippery roads:
  power skids, 68
  single-car accidents, 23
  speed and stopping distance, 31, 86
  (see also Icy roads; Snowy roads;
    Wet roads)
Slowing vehicles, collisions with, 23
Smoking, 122
Snow:
  avoiding driving in, 79
  clearing from windows and mirrors,
    79
  freeing car from, 100-101
Snow tires, 99, 100, 167
Snowy roads, 79, 81, 82
  speed and stopping distance, 31
Society of Automotive Engineers, 58,
    67
Spare tire, 167
Spark plugs, 167
Speed:
  addictiveness of, 126, 132
  adjusting to range of headlights, 122
  and centrifugal force, 60
  for cornering, 75, 79
  excessive, accidents due to, 61
  and G-forces, 59, 60-63, 173
  and handling, 105-7
  on icy roads, 82
  and limit of adhesion, 53
  miles per hour v. feet per second,
    30-31, 176
  and stopping distance, 31-32, 85-86,
    108, 134
  and time saved, 32
  and tire pressure, 97
  and tire wear, 97
  tracking, in high-speed pursuit,
    141-42
  and vehicle control, 30-32
  on wet roads, 81
  (see also High-speed driving)
Speed changes:
  to avoid head-on collision, 24
  driving exercises, 104-7
  erratic, due to fatigue, 13
  sudden, 26
  and vehicle dynamics, 48
Speed limit, exceeding, 139, 140, 156